Princess Mentality

Ready to Reign

LaToya NaShae

Table of Contents

Part Three: Purpose 68

Part Four: Promise 106

Hey Hun!

First, welcome! I'm too excited that you decided to embark on this journey of mind renewal. Way to go! Salvation is not just the end of the old you; it is the beginning of a life of boundless freedom in Christ! *Whom the Son sets free is free INDEED!* (John 8:36). You, my dear, are free. Nah, boo. Don't just shake your head in agreement. It's time to live like you *really* know WHOSE you are!

Allow me to warn you in advance. The questions are hard-hitting. Group discussions are designed to reach far beyond the surface. We ready ourselves to reign by getting to the root of things. And let me tell you, there WILL be some uprooting! That's why we're here, right? We are determined to live unstuck, unbound, unbreakable lives in Christ!

Together, we will embrace the smiles and tears, the woo-sah and ah-ha moments. We aren't just going through each section; we are *growing* through Position, Power, Purpose, and Promise. During this journey, we will be respectfully raw, real, and relevant. Transparency and vulnerability do not intimidate us to the point of silence. Strength is in numbers, so let's walk this thing out... together.

Sincerely,

LaToya NaShae

What to Expect

- *Princess Mentality: Ready to Reign* is comprised of 4 parts: Position, Power, Purpose, and Promise. Each part contains 4 corresponding chapters.

- Each of the 4 parts begins with a *Mentality Challenge*. These questions help to identify potential areas for growth and initiate the process of mind renewal.

- Every section ends with a *Mentality Shift*. You will be challenged to rethink some things! Space is allotted for each question to be answered in detail. The more effort put into these journal activities, the more growth you will experience.

- Although *Princess Mentality* can be read individually, it is strongly encouraged that you work through the content in a small group setting or with a few like-minded friends.

- Stretching is uncomfortable. Allow yourself to be stretched anyway. Life transformation begins in the mind. Commit to the process of developing a princess mentality.

INTRODUCTION

Dismantling Distortion

Once upon a time, before the earth was formed or light found its shine, God thought of you with loving kindness. Before you were conceived in your mother's womb, you were conceived in His heart. His intent was to give you hope and a future that coincided with living out the fullness of His Word. Then, along came the tempter.

Every fairy tale has its villain, but this is no bedtime saga. This is reality – *your* reality. The threat of the adversary is real. God's will was never for you to become distant, but darkness crept in and you lost your way for some time. Intimate fellowship between the two of you was always the Father's objective. For reasons beyond your control, humanity entered into a perverted love affair with the wicked one. You became the prisoner of an invisible war. Curses were never supposed to prevail, but generation after generation has chosen to dwell in the land of disobedience and forfeit their blessed inheritance. Now, you are uncertain of where here is and confused about who you are supposed to be.

Rest assured that confusion is not God's will. His desire was for you to experience life and abundantly so. That desire hasn't changed. Just as you were in His heart before time began, so was a plan for redemption. Since you have believed in your heart and confessed with your mouth that Jesus is Lord, you have been reconciled to God by the Blood. Ayyye! You're brand new, boo!

This isn't make-believe, but there is a miraculous ending in which justice will be served and happily ever after will be experienced. Until then, there is life to be lived and purpose to be carried out. For far too long, you have strained to see hope. Your identity has been compromised. Your vision has been skewed by loss, disappointment, and fear. Hun, that simply won't do! Do you know who your Daddy is? Do you know Who created you?

It's time for a shift in your thinking. It's time for clarity and revelation. It's time for you to claim your position as a daughter of the Almighty God. Your Father is the King. As a result of this royal relationship, you have been given the mind of Christ. It's time for you to break away from faithless mental limitations and don the mentality of a princess. Let the journey begin...

[14] But people who aren't spiritual can't receive these truths from God's Spirit. It all sounds foolish to them and they can't understand it, for only those who are spiritual can understand what the Spirit means. [15] Those who are spiritual can evaluate all things, but they themselves cannot be evaluated by others. [16] For, "Who can know the Lord's thoughts? Who knows enough to teach him?" But we understand these things, for we have the mind of Christ. I Corinthians 2:14-16, NLT

Mentality Challenge: Position

Describe your current mentality.

Who has God purposed you to be?

What do you believe is the internal disconnect between where you are and who you are destined to be?

PART ONE
Position

Fact: *Whose* you are determines *who* you are.

Hun, you are *precisely* where you should be. No, no. Not particularly as it relates to your circumstances. This is so much deeper than that. Expand your frame of focus beyond this natural realm. Yes, you are in this world, but you *are not* of it. You are a spiritual being, currently housed in a temporal body, taking part in an earthly existence that is very much a soul experience. That's a mouthful, right? Life as you know it is being assessed based on your mind, will, and emotions. The world around you is filtered daily through your senses, past experiences, and current mood. Think on this: How could a shift in thinking cause you to imagine beyond that which is apparent? There's no time like the present to change things up a bit. To be different, you must think differently. Broaden your mind to envision possibilities of greater.

But it is written, Eye has not seen, nor ear heard, neither have entered into the heart of man, the things which God has prepared for them that love Him. I Corinthians 2:9

Take the limits off! Where you are in terms of geographic location pales in comparison to who you are in Christ. It is God who designs your life's path and directs you along the way. And, oh, what a marvelous path it is! *In His presence there is fullness of joy and pleasures forevermore.* (Psalm 16:11). IN HIS PRESENCE. [*She*] *that dwells in the Secret Place of the Most High shall abide under the shadow of the Almighty.* (Psalm 91:1). Whose you are is indicative of who you are, where you are, where you are going, and what you will do. Ooh, chile. That's a lot to process! Take some time to digest these truths, and then we will continue.

Being a child of God means you are a daughter of El Elyon, God Most High, and a joint-heir with Christ. You are positioned for greatness. You are positioned and predestined to bear *much* fruit as you abide in the presence of your Father, the King.

[1] I will lift up my eyes to the hills – from whence comes my help? [2] My help comes from the Lord, who made heaven and earth. Psalm 121:1-2

Stop looking around believing you are supposed to be anywhere but here. This is your place of breakthrough. Now is when you BREAKOUT! You are on the cusp of the season for which you have been praying. Vision is required to recognize the blessing attached to your position. Look to Jesus, the author and finisher of your faith. The past is fixed; there is no changing it. Stop mentally dwelling in yesterday. Today comes equipped with empowering grace. Hope is the reason for rising with joy tomorrow. By way of the Holy Spirit, God heals the scars of your past, comforts and counsels you in the present, and lights the way for the days to come. His Word is true: *the Lord shall preserve your going out and your coming in from this time forth, and even forevermore.* (Psalm 121:8). Focus forward by faith as your future unfolds. You are where you are supposed to be – poised and positioned in the presence of the King.

Dear Princess, you have been deemed royalty for such a time as this. Greatness has been planted within you; His name is the Holy Spirit. Ahead is a path of discovery that extends beyond these pages and translates into real life. The Word wasn't just meant for recitation and meditation; it applies to everyday life. It was given to be loved and lived. For *in the beginning was the Word, and the Word was with God, and the Word was God...And the Word was made flesh, and dwelt among us, (and we beheld His glory, the glory as of the only begotten of the Father,) full of grace and truth.* (John 1:1, 14). To love God is to lovingly embrace His Son and live out His Word.

Lord, give your daughter eyes to see, ears to hear, a heart to believe, a voice that sincerely says, "send me", and feet that will go without hesitation. Light her way with Your Word of Truth. May her faith increase as she calls the realities of heaven down to earth. Give her the grace to be all that You have ordained her to be. In Jesus' name, amen.

Chapter One
You ARE the Father

A publicly televised paternity test won't be necessary. There is no need for a stage or rowdy crowd. Side-by-side pictures to convince onlookers of similar facial features won't be required. No ma'am! There will be none of *that*! This Daddy is not in denial; you were made in His image. This Father proudly calls you His own. Court ordered visitation isn't necessary; this Father is never far away. He inhabits the praises of His people. No trickery is needed to persuade Him to sign your birth certificate. Dear one, He lovingly engrafted you into His family at the point of salvation. Christ's Blood was the only signature needed. GOD IS YOUR FATHER.

By the works of His hands you were formed, and surely He makes no mistakes. You are His workmanship, His creation. Oh, to be loved and claimed by the Father! However sketchy your past may be, He calls you fearfully and wonderfully made. So what's causing you to doubt? Looking over your shoulder, I presume.

Newsflash: Your backstory doesn't matter. Where you come from, the things you have done, and those ungodly connections that once served as the chains linking you to your former sinful nature no longer have any bearing on your current position. HE IS YOUR FATHER. Settle that in your heart. You have been born again; you've been made new.

Therefore, if anyone is in Christ, [she] is a new creation; old things have passed away; behold, all things have become new. II Corinthians 5:17

Anyone. That includes you. Old things have passed away. Rejoice, for you have been made new! His Spirit bears witness with your spirit; beyond any doubt, you are a child of God (see Romans 8:16). The distinct mark of His presence is upon you. Normal? Nah, boo. You are far from ordinary or basic. *But you are a chosen generation, a royal priesthood, a holy nation, His own special people, that you may proclaim the praises of Him who called you out of darkness into His marvelous light.* (I Peter 2:9). Simply put, you are a special edition. That is something to shout about! Grasp hold of this truth: You are called to stand out, separated from darkness and set aside for works of righteousness. God declares that you are exceptional... and rightfully so. He is the King of kings and the Lord of lords. You are His daughter, a princess of the divine sort.

Let the weightiness of this revelation sink into your spirit until you are fully persuaded that you have been embraced by God. He chose you to carry out His good works in the earth as a vessel of honor. Free your mind of every thought that dares to challenge your position in the kingdom. Understand that *if anyone purifies [herself] from anything dishonorable, [she] will be a special instrument, set apart, useful to the Master, prepared for every good work.* (II Timothy 2:20-21, HCSB). Wait! Before the pressure of perfection overtakes you, find relief in knowing that the process of sanctification – simply put, becoming more and more like Jesus – is not carried out in our own strength or by a personal definition of righteousness. The Holy Spirit leads you in all truth. As you yield to His guidance, purification occurs. Whew! Wipe the sweat from your brow. You aren't expected to be perfect, only obedient.

I have been crucified with Christ; it is no longer I who live, but Christ lives in me; and the life which I now live in the flesh I live by faith in the Son of God, who loved me and gave Himself for me. Galatians 2:20

You have simultaneously been placed in a position of life and death. To live, you must die. When you agreed to relinquish the throne of your heart to Christ, you signed up for daily suicide. Nobody told you? Yes, 'tis true. Selfish ambition, personal gratification, and previous agendas that are not pleasing to God must go! This isn't a compromise of your uniqueness. On the contrary, you are blessed with the opportunity to discover who you were truly created to be. To adopt a princess mentality, the old mindset along with its inhibitions must go. You aren't losing yourself; you're finding yourself *in Him*. Perspective is the key.

To fully walk in the privilege and power vested in you, introspection is required. *[23] Search me, O God, and know my heart; try me, and know my anxieties; [24] and see if there is any wicked way in me, and lead me in the way everlasting.* (Psalm 139:23-24). That's a mighty, courageous prayer, don't you think? To make such a bold petition, to dare to ask God to reveal those nook and cranny vices of yours, takes faith. Wonderful! You meet the prerequisite! According to Ephesians 2:8, *you have been saved by grace THROUGH faith.* The very fact that God is now your Father means you have exactly what's needed to go before the throne of grace and ask that He reveal those old lingering traits that are preventing you from fully walking in the newness that has been granted. You have the faith-backed courage to pray, "Dear Lord, shine Your light on the remaining residue of my past. Cleanse me from every sin and stumbling block that prevents a closer walk with You."

Have no fear, He'll do just that. Or do you fear that He *will* do it? There is fear in taking off the masks and pulling back the layers, correct? There is vulnerability in transparency. The thought of being naked and unashamed is so foreign. There is danger in being fully exposed, right? Actually, there isn't. This fact may have slipped your mind, but we will rehearse it until it is ingrained in your very being: HE IS YOUR FATHER. Nothing in this world – or outside of it for that matter – could make Him stop loving you. What is the fear in asking Him to show you the dark parts of your heart that He already plainly sees? Right; He is completely aware of your every shortcoming, yet He loves you anyway. This is a Daddy unlike one you've ever known. Open up and be transparent. It is for your good and His glory.

The resistance you're experiencing is normal. But remember, you aren't normal anymore. Prior to your spiritual acceptance, it was necessary to construct emotional walls. That's how you survived. Again, the old things have passed away. Formerly you survived, now you have been positioned to thrive. Remove the masks. You don't have to have it all figured out. He will prepare you for the seasons of shifting that are to come. The Lord will perfect that which concerns you. His mercy is unending; He wouldn't dare forsake the work of His hands (see Psalm 138:8). Do away with the skepticism. He is faithful enough to protect you. Instead of crumbling under truth, you will rise with a new found freedom that results from darkness giving way to light. *The name of the Lord is a strong tower; the righteous run to it and are safe.* (Proverbs 18:10). Don't flee from His presence. Go deeper.

It's tempting, right? I know. It sounds... nice... and liberating... but. There are a million buts. Regardless of your excuse, God is unchanging. He was faithful enough to offer you salvation; will He not continue in the way of faithfulness as He transforms you into the similitude of His Son? No matter how ill-prepared or unequipped you may think you are, He is well able to provide every resource needed for this journey of faith. This is child support to the exponential degree! *God shall supply all your need according to His riches and glory by Christ Jesus.* (Philippians 4:19). Nothing about that verse is dependent on you. Your duty is to receive. You are the apple of His eye, His precious one. You are positioned for greatness. Your destiny is in His will. Don't be intimidated. This is doable; however, mind renewal is essential for life renovation. You are a daughter of the King; He formed you for such a time as this. Your life has purpose. Will you trust Him to shift your thinking beyond current limitations? Your tiara is the mind of Christ. Will you don it daily? Are you willing to step out in faith – regardless of the challenges that may arise? It's scary, I know. Committing to something without knowing all the particulars isn't recommended in the natural, but this is the stuff faith is made of. Fear will subside as faith arises for *God has not given you a spirit of fear; but of power, and of love, and of a sound mind.* (II Timothy 2:7). He is well able to prepare, protect, and provide.

There is no need to fortify your heart against the Father. He is *for* you, not against you. Will you pull down your barriers? He doesn't deny you at all. Will you receive His acceptance? Perhaps you're unsure about His expectations. Let me help you. You know what He wants? He wants others to see Him when they look at you. He wants believers and unbelievers alike to see you and say HE IS HER FATHER.

Chapter Two
Time Out for Prim & Proper

⁹ As we have said before, so now I say again, if anyone preaches any other gospel to you than what you have received, let him be accursed. ¹⁰ For do I now persuade men, or God? Or do I seek to please men? For if I still pleased men, I would not be a bondservant of Christ. Galatians 1:9-10

Let's cut to the chase, shall we? All things are to be done decently and in order, but the world has infiltrated the Church in an effort to redefine its decency and order. Princess, that simply should not be! Who defines God's Word but God? Who is qualified to rightly divide His Word of Truth except His children who walk according to His Spirit? Your reign as a daughter of the Most High provides a platform for holy boldness. To what extent will righteousness be compromised for the sake of remaining politically correct?

To be a bondservant of Christ is to have Him as your Lord – fully surrendered and serving no other. To know Christ as Lord is to accept His Word as first priority and final authority. Your heart isn't divided and your worship is sincere. You find rest in His sovereignty and courage in His light. You are victorious because Christ has gone before you. Yet a war is being waged for your destiny and desires, your voice and vision, your image and influence. Now is not the time for double-mindedness. Focus and tap into your holy boldness.

"You are the salt of the earth; but if the salt loses its flavor, how shall it be seasoned? It is then good for nothing but to be thrown out and trampled underfoot by men. Matthew 5:13

Complacency leads to a sugary-sweet, "come as you are/stay as you are" religious fallacy that wars against true intimacy with God. To walk with God is to walk with His Word, for God and His Word are one. The Word was never meant to conveniently fit into our lives, but to bring transformation and be our source of life. The Word is meant to change us not vice versa. For it is written, *16All Scripture is given by inspiration of God, and is profitable for doctrine, for reproof, for correction, for instruction in righteousness, 17 that the man of God may be complete, thoroughly equipped for every good work.* (II Timothy 3:16-17). Thorough. Complete. Fully equipped.

The Word wasn't given to be watered down; neither have you been placed in this generation to have your voice silenced. You have been called to shine as a light in the darkness. Influence has been granted. Your good works are needed so *others will see them and glorify your Father which is in heaven.* (Matthew 5:16). The standard to which you have been summoned exceeds that of this world's morality. Does that calling permit a judgmental spirit? Absolutely not!

[1]"Judge not, that you be not judged. [2] For with what judgment you judge, you will be judged; and with the measure you use, it will be measured back to you. [3] And why do you look at the speck in your brother's eye, but do not consider the plank in your own eye? [4] Or how can you say to your brother, 'Let me remove the speck from your eye'; and look, a plank is in your own eye? [5] Hypocrite! First remove the plank from your own eye, and then you will see clearly to remove the speck from your brother's eye. Matthew 7:1-5

Simply put, sweep around your own front door. Examine *your* heart. Deal with the issues of darkness that remain in *your* life. You see, there is only One fit to judge, but instead He has chosen to love. Rather than unleashing wrath, He extends mercy. *For God did not send His Son into the world to condemn the world, but that the world through Him might be saved.* (John 3:17). The final judgment could have been decreed when Christ came to earth. Instead, He went to the Cross so that we could taste and see the goodness of the Lord. The veil was torn – no more separation between the Father and us. How dare we be critical of others when God's love toward us has been so unconditional! Even still, to be one who extends grace is not the equivalent of disregarding sin. Accepting one's sin is not a requirement for loving them. Are you in need of proof? Let's review God's Word.

[43] For a good tree does not bear bad fruit, nor does a bad tree bear good fruit. [44] For every tree is known by its own fruit. For men do not gather figs from thorns, nor do they gather grapes from a bramble bush. Luke 6:43-44

Open rebuke is better than love carefully concealed. Proverbs 27:5

As iron sharpens iron, so a [woman] sharpens the countenance of [her] friend. Proverbs 27:17

Let the word of Christ dwell in you richly in all wisdom, teaching and admonishing one another in psalms and hymns and spiritual songs, singing with grace in your hearts to the Lord. Colossians 3:16

Acknowledge the fruit, but don't judge the bearer. Love the lost, but don't dull your shine to accommodate their sinful nature. Extend grace, but don't shy away from the fact that *the wages of sin is death.* (Romans 6:23) What am I saying? Be clothed in Christ so that His light radiates from within, causing your life to speak in a way more effectively life-changing than words. Be influential. Ungodliness comes at a price far too steep for anyone to afford. Have you stopped to consider the duplicity in claiming to care about someone yet not encouraging him or her to lead a godly life? How does one do so without wagging a finger or stepping on toes? It's simple: lead by example.

Imitate me, just as I also imitate Christ. I Corinthians 11:1

God isn't asking for your perfection but rather your availability. As He sanctifies you, you will be met with opportunities to pour into others. The call of every Spirit-filled believer is to make disciples. Not only are we to introduce the lost to Christ but also to teach them how to live for Him.

The Spirit will teach you to be a teacher. He will guide you into all truth and understanding as you guide others. Who will you bless? Who will you train to live for the Lord? Elijah mentored Elisha. Paul was a spiritual father to Timothy. And it's not just a "man thing". Naomi taught Ruth a thing or two and Elizabeth encouraged Mary, the mother of Jesus. You have something to offer. You can be of service to the kingdom of God. Perhaps you are still puzzled by the "how".

7 But the end of all things is at hand; therefore be serious and watchful in your prayers. 8 And above all things have fervent love for one another, for "love will cover a multitude of sins." 9 Be hospitable to one another without grumbling.10 As each one has received a gift, minister it to one another, as good stewards of the manifold grace of God. I Peter 4:7-10

Be loving. Be gracious. Extend mercy. See beyond the sin and seek to minister to the heart of broken individuals. The Holy Spirit, our divine Teacher, guides us in learning to love the sinner while standing firm against sin. Commit this to memory: unconditional love inspires change while harsh criticism evokes resistance. A judgmental approach is made ineffective by the conflict it produces and the love that it lacks. Genuine concern speaks to the heart of a person; it recognizes their good despite their flaws. The message of Christ was love and redemption, not condemnation and wrath. Hopeless, despondent, rejected, bitter – the lost come with an array of problems, but Christ is their one solution. Will you be their guiding light?

7 So you, son of man: I have made you a watchman for the house of Israel; therefore you shall hear a word from My mouth and warn them for Me. 8 When I say to the wicked, 'O wicked man, you shall surely die!' and you do not speak to warn the wicked from his way, that wicked man shall die in his iniquity; but his blood I will require at your hand. ⁹ Nevertheless if you warn the wicked to turn from his way, and he does not turn from his way, he shall die in his iniquity; but you have delivered your soul. Ezekiel 33:7-9

Our sobering reality is that the clock is ticking. No man knows the day or hour of Christ's return, but all signs point to soon. Have you stopped to consider that co-worker who sleeps in every Sunday or that family member who lost his faith after a series of life-altering events? Their souls are on the line...and you are connected to the Lifeline they desperately but unknowingly need. Will you sound the alarm? Will you bring light to their dark world? Will you boldly live out your faith or quietly pray that God sends someone in your place?

And do not be conformed to this world, but be transformed by the renewing of your mind so that you may prove what is that good and acceptable and perfect will of God. Romans 12:2

Stand out, dear one, stand out! Dare to be different. By the Blood, you are saved and sanctified to shatter the confines of the status quo. As society redefines right and wrong, you must be the one to stand firm on God's unchanging Word. Some will criticize; others will follow your example. You are brave enough to unapologetically live out the Word of Truth. You weren't created for timidity. No ma'am! *God has not given you a spirit of fear, but of power and of love and of a sound mind.* (II Timothy 1:7). Shake off fear and insecurity. Access the power of the Holy Spirit Who lives in you. Radiate the love that has been so graciously shed upon your life. Your personality makes an impact. Your voice has listeners. You have God-ordained influence. Don't step back. STAND OUT.

Chapter Three
Purposed to Reflect

Are you struggling to see how all of this will play out? It sounds good, being positioned as God's child and made a princess by the Blood. All of that is great in theory. However, it's difficult to envision how this concept plays out in real life. The truth is you aren't blinded by the bling of a tiara when you look in the mirror; you just see you. No one is bowing in your presence or tending to your every beck and call. Millions aren't following you as you follow Christ. You are *just* you.

STOP. Let me get you together. Boo, there is nothing *just* about you. God, who knows you, knows that you are divinely amazing. Your struggle results from having limited pieces of the puzzle, whereas He sees the whole picture. He says you are fearfully and wonderfully made. Your doubt dares to counter that notion. *How can I be wonderful and a work in progress at the same time?* Trust His assessment. All things are possible to she who believes.

[12] Now we see things imperfectly, like puzzling reflections in a mirror, but then we will see everything with perfect clarity. All that I know now is partial and incomplete, but then I will know everything completely, just as God now knows me completely. [13] Three things will last forever—faith, hope, and love—and the greatest of these is love. I Corinthians 13:12-13, NLT

Perhaps you can't see it, but there is more to come – deeper fellowship with your Creator, greater revelation of His truths, transition sprinkled with adversity, and growth through it all. It continues to get greater. Becoming new is a process. The Potter invests time to skilfully craft you into all that He created you to be. It's a process. Though there is a chip here and a scratch there, He still sees fit to use you while in transition. His will is to work on *and* through you as you remain on the wheel. You can simultaneously walk in purpose and be under construction. What a resourceful God we serve!

In the sweet by and by you will behold the glory of God and be perfected in His presence. Here and now you have the distinguished privilege and responsibility of living for His glory. You are positioned to reflect the image of Christ. You have hope in the steadfast love of God, knowing that although you have yet to become the you who will reside with Him for all of eternity, you still bear His image in the earth.

17 Now the Lord is the Spirit, and where the Spirit of the Lord is, there is liberty (emancipation from bondage, freedom). 18 And all of us, as with unveiled face, [because we] continued to behold [in the Word of God] as in a mirror the glory of the Lord, are constantly being transfigured into His very own image in ever increasing splendor and from one degree of glory to another; [for this comes] from the Lord [Who is] the Spirit. II Corinthians 3:17-18, Amplified

No Windex needed; a crystal-clear image of the life and legacy of Christ has been presented to you. There is no veil. The Ark of the Covenant once housed the presence of God, but now you are His chosen temple. Where His Spirit is, there is liberty. As you walk in the freedom granted to you, understand that you are encountering new levels of glory. You don't have to know all the details; simply trust that His thoughts toward you are good and that a favored future full of kingdom-building awaits you.

So, my dear [sisters], be strong and immovable. Always work enthusiastically for the Lord, for you know that nothing you do for the Lord is ever useless. I Corinthians 15:58, NLT

4 Now there are diversities of gifts, but the same Spirit. 5 And there are differences of administrations, but the same Lord. 6 And there are diversities of operations, but it is the same God which

worketh all in all. ⁷ But the manifestation of the Spirit is given to every man to profit withal. I Corinthians 12:4-7

Daughter of God, you are being transformed into the image of Christ this very moment. This process has purpose and your purpose has spiritual gifts attached to it. Whatever your gift may be, it is *for the perfecting of the saints, for the work of the ministry, and for the edifying of the Body of Christ.* (Ephesians 4:12). The image of Christ is reflected as you flow in your calling.

Jesus prayed to the Father, *That they all may be one: as You, Father, are in Me, and I in You, that they also may be one in Us: that the world may believe that You have sent Me. And the glory which You gave Me I have given them; that they may be one, even as we are One.* (John 17:22). You aren't in this alone. You haven't been assigned to a solo shine mission. To belong to Christ is to be grafted into the Body. Unity brings the blessings of God. It causes us to set aside differences to carry the Gospel of Christ to a dying world. To be one Body with many members requires the knitting together of hearts for one purpose: be a disciplined follower of the Lord Jesus Christ.

³⁴ A new commandment I give to you, That you love one another; as I have loved you, that you also love one another. ³⁵ By this shall all men know that you are My disciples, if you have love one to another. John 13:34-35

More than operating in a gift or talent, attending church or performing good works, love is the tell-tale sign that Christ has captured your heart. That is not to say that those things aren't important, but to walk in love is to reflect His heart. When love is the central focus, peace is the standard, unity is the aim, and you extend grace as it is extended to you. If love is your motivation, the rest will be customary. Your conversations will be seasoned with salt and your life will be as a city upon a hill.

Love is truly the answer for the world today. That sounds cliché, but it is so very true. As a child of God, you are a change agent in the earth. You are purposed to have the love of God shed abroad in your heart. Love is the light that drives out darkness. Be that light. It restores hope to the hopeless and helps the lost to find their way. Give hope; provide direction. God is love. And you, dear one, are the lovely vessel through which He intends to mend hearts. Walk in your purpose. Reflect the love of God.

Chapter Four
Legitimately Sealed

26 But you do not believe, because you are not of My sheep, as I said to you. 27 My sheep hear My voice, and I know them, and they follow Me. 28 And I give them eternal life, and they shall never perish; neither shall anyone snatch them out of My hand.
John 10:26-18

You are His sheep. You hear and believe by faith. My sister, without a doubt, you are His. How sweet it is to be loved by Jesus! You have never known this kind of security. Your spot is solidified. It is legitimately established by Kingdom rules and principles. *If you confess with your mouth the Lord Jesus and believe in your heart that God has raised Him from the dead, you will be saved.* (Romans 10:9). You've done that, correct? Then your life is hidden in Christ and no one can snatch you from His presence. This seems so unnatural. You have never experienced such assurance. Correct! This is supernatural! There is no greater title to bear on earth than child of God. And it's yours! There isn't a need to work for your position; it is yours. Simply work your position.

¹ What then shall we say that Abraham our father has found according to the flesh? ² For if Abraham was justified by works, he has something to boast about, but not before God. ³ For what does the Scripture say? "Abraham believed God, and it was accounted to him for righteousness." ⁴ Now to him who works, the wages are not counted as grace but as debt. ⁵ But to him who does not work but believes on Him who justifies the ungodly, his faith is accounted for righteousness. Romans 4:1-5

God spoke; Abraham believed and was deemed righteous because of his faith. God has spoken; you believed for salvation and by the Blood of Christ you have been gifted with righteousness. Are you perfect? No. Are you righteous? Yes. Did you earn it? Nope! Christ paid the price for you; walk in it. Does that sound too easy? Stay with me; we're going somewhere.

Although faith without works is dead, works don't earn your relationship with Christ. They are a result of intimate fellowship with Him. A sincere heart does not desire to frustrate the grace of God. Those who worship in spirit and in truth understand that there is no separation between love and obedience. The old you has been put away and Christ now lives through you. Your position is this: The Spirit of Christ is in you and you are in Christ. Glory to God!

You work your position by submitting to the will of the Lord. There is no spiritual corporate ladder to climb. Be you – the daughter God created you to be. Biblical mind renewal brings understanding. We are accustomed to making a name for ourselves, but the only name that deserves to be exalted is Christ's. Good works are a byproduct of a surrendered life. God's system of dying to live and operating in humility is such a contradiction to a natural life of self-promotion and paper chasing. God's kingdom is different. All thanks be to God for His ways are not our ways! There is no competition or point to prove. Let it be stated once more for emphasis: you don't work *for* your position, instead *work* your position. Be the woman God has called you to be by walking confidently in your identity. You, my sister, were born to reign as a lady of light. Embrace your position.

20 For all the promises of God in Him are Yes, and in Him Amen, to the glory of God through us. 21 Now He who establishes us with you in Christ and has anointed us is God, 22 who also has sealed us and given us the Spirit in our hearts as a guarantee. II Corinthians 1:20-22

You are established and anointed. The Word says it. Will you believe? The Holy Spirit sealed the deal and your heart is His dwelling place. Yes, you house the presence of the living God. Take a moment to meditate on the power of that truth.

You are perfectly placed in the kingdom to be a conduit through which power flows. The anointing *is* power, and you have been empowered to carry out the work of Jesus. *Most assuredly, I say to you, he who believes in Me, the works that I do he will do also; and greater works than these he will do, because I go to My Father.* (John 14:12). Jesus spoke it, so believe it.

Every promise outlined in the Word of God is yours based on divine positioning. Are you in need of healing? *By His stripes you are healed.* (Isaiah 53:5). Is it a struggle to see yourself as God sees you? No worries! *Come boldly unto the throne of grace, that you may obtain mercy, and grace to help you in time of need.* (Hebrews 4:16). Perhaps the heaviness of your heart cannot be articulated. *The Spirit also helps in our weaknesses. For we do not know what we should pray for as we ought, but the Spirit Himself makes intercession for us with groanings which cannot be uttered.* (Romans 8:26). The origin of your struggle may be dwindling faith; it just doesn't seem as if you have enough to see manifestation. Okay. There is Word to combat that as well. *If you have faith as a mustard seed, you will say to this mountain, 'Move from here to there,' and it will move; and nothing will be impossible for you.* (Matthew 17:20).

The enemy's goal is to have you hemmed up, wrestling with doubt and insecurity. By the authority given to you, cast down every thought that dares to exalt itself against the word that God has spoken over your life. Speak the Word! Command the enemy to get under your feet! Who dares to curse the daughter whom God has blessed? When God is for you, it doesn't matter who chooses to be against you.

[She] who dwells in the Secret Place of the Most High shall abide under the Shadow of the Almighty. Psalm 91:1

Settle this in your heart today: the promises of God for you are yes and amen. (See II Corinthians 1:20). Abide. Your sufficiency is in God. That means your entitlement is a result of being His child. Rest under the shelter of His wings. There is freedom in having a heartfelt understanding of Whose you are. You are privileged by association, positioned to humbly follow Christ.

Mentality Shift: Position

Chapter One

What emotions do you associate with cultivating an intimate relationship with the Father? Describe the thoughts associated with these emotions.

Chapter Two

Define accountability and transparency in your own words. How do these words factor into discipleship?

Chapter Three

In what ways are you most like your Heavenly Father? How are you different?

Chapter Four

God designed us to feel remorse over sin in order to produce repentance that leads to victor. This leaves us with no regrets. But the sorrow of the world works death. II Corinthians 7:10, TPT

How has worldly sorrow hindered your faith?

Mentality Challenge: Power

When do you feel most pressured to conform to the world's standards?

How does fear cause you to become complacent?

Every act of God is intertwined with purpose, including your creation. There is a reason for the power you possess. Who is God empowering you to empower?

PART TWO
Power

Fact: The Power Source to which you are connected is a never-ending spiritual supply.

21 So Jesus said to them again, "Peace to you! As the Father has sent Me, I also send you." 22 And when He had said this, He breathed on them, and said to them, "Receive the Holy Spirit. John 20:21-22

Breathe on Your child, O God, that she may know the comforting weight of Your presence and the indwelling of Your Spirit.

Hun, inhale the Way, the Truth, and the Life. Exhale love, joy, peace, patience, kindness, goodness, faithfulness, gentleness, and self-control. Receive the seed of God's Word into the soil of your heart, and produce the fruit of the Spirit in your everyday life.

Lord, thank You for the breath of life. This gift You give is not in vain. I ask that You direct Your daughter in the way that she should go, because surely You have empowered her to do so. May her heart always be sensitive to Your leading as You teach her to flow in the power that has been bestowed upon her. Guide her in being extraordinary even in the ordinary.

And so, dear brothers and sisters, I plead with you to give your bodies to God because of all He has done for you. Let them be a living and holy sacrifice—the kind He will find acceptable. This is truly the way to worship Him. ² Don't copy the behavior and customs of this world, but let God transform you into a new person by changing the way you think. Then you will learn to know God's will for you, which is good and pleasing and perfect. Romans 12:1-2, NLT

Realize that Monday through Sunday are days the Lord has made. Rejoice and be glad, boo! He is the God of your every day. As the sun rises to introduce another twenty-four hours, offer yourself to God in honor of your risen Savior. Being a walking, talking, constant praise-giving, in-spirit-and-in-truth worshipping sacrifice is your reasonable service.

Don't blend in, STAND OUT! Give yourself to Him wholly. You are ordained to be different, set up to be set apart. The darkness and shadows of today's culture will not overtake your light, for the radiance of Christ shines from within you.

As God sent Christ, so is Christ sending you. Where shall you go? Wherever He leads. What will you do? Whatever He commands. Does fear threaten to overtake you? Quite possibly. However, *God has not given you a spirit of fear; but of power, love, and a sound mind.* (II Timothy 1:7). Therefore, *be strong and of a good courage; do not be afraid or dismayed: for the Lord your God is with you WHEREVER you go.* (Joshua 1:8).

You are strengthened to go where the Spirit leads, appointed to represent the name of the Lord, and free to be precisely who God has purposed you to be. Operate in the power you've been given.

Chapter Five
Warrior Princess

BOOM! Life threw a mighty blow; now you're dazed and confused. POW! There goes another unexpected curve ball. WHAT IN THE WORLD? You are a Word-speaking, faith-walking child of God. You do not deserve this! Precisely, boo!

Reality Check: You have an adversary whose goal is to render you ineffective in every possible way.

The enemy lurks about waiting for the most opportune time to strike. He studies your words and actions for any inkling of weakness. He's watching. Nevertheless, don't shrink back in terror. Don't look around; look up. The pressure is on, but you are an overcomer. Shake off the anxiety that dares to overtake you. *⁶Be anxious for nothing, but in everything by prayer and supplication, with thanksgiving, let your requests be made known to God; ⁷ and the peace of God, which surpasses all understanding, will guard your hearts and minds through Christ Jesus.* (Philippians 4:6-7). Yes! Grab hold to that peace and steady your mind. Assume a posture of triumph. Even when you don't feel like it, victory is yours. *Greater is He that is in you than he that is in the world.* (I John 4:4). It is the He that is in you that the he of this world loathes.

12 Beloved, do not think it strange concerning the fiery trial which is to try you, as though some strange thing happened to you; 13 but rejoice to the extent that you partake of Christ's sufferings, that when His glory is revealed, you may also be glad with exceeding joy. I Peter 4:12-14

Every storm won't be self-inflicted. You know that. Bad things sometimes happen to good people, but rejoice in suffering? Come again. How is it even possible to *count it all joy when you fall into various trials?* (James 2:2). The key is to continue reading: *3 Knowing that the testing of your faith produces patience. 4 But let patience have its perfect work, that you may be perfect and complete, lacking nothing.* (James 2:3-4).

While there is nothing glorious about the thought of going through, you must understand that when you trust the Holy Spirit to navigate you to the other side of hardship, you come out stronger, wiser, and more deeply rooted in your faith. You are being perfected through this process.

Prissy, pampered princess – that you are not! Hun, *even though Jesus was God's Son, He learned obedience from the things He suffered.* (Hebrews 5:8, NLT). Whew! Hard times hit differently when you consider all that Christ endured. Jesus went through some things, and now He is seated at the right hand of the Father where He makes intercession on your behalf. Not only does He pray for you, He has endowed you with His Spirit to ensure the building of your testimony with every test. What an thorough God we serve!

Princess, this is not the time or place for a pity party. The position and power of which you are currently privileged to partake is a direct result of the sufferings of Christ. Who will reap a blessing from the burden you bear? It is written, *they overcame him by the Blood of the Lamb, and by the word of their testimony, and they did not love their lives to the death.* (Revelation 12:11). Selfishness advises you to run for cover and save yourself. Christ has done all the saving that's needed. Fear has no place in your heart. Your misery can birth a glorious ministry. There is purpose in this pressing place. Satan cannot defeat you for you have been strengthened for such a time as this. Let the warrior spirit within you arise.

Chapter Six
Arrayed and Ready

For you were once darkness, but now you are light in the Lord. Walk as children of light. Ephesians 5:8

Shine, boo! Blaze bright for the Son! Once you danced with darkness and caressed compromise, but light is now your dwelling place. An inward transformation has produced an outward manifestation. You are different. You look the same, but you are different. Godly garments – those that can be witnessed but not seen – are very becoming to you. From head to toe, you are on point! You seem to not have realized it, but trust me; one glance of the spiritual eye and it's clear what you're about: Kingdom business.

Your Father fashioned you as a fierce and favored fashionista. You didn't know? Hun-neeey, yes! The saintly styles He has prepared for you are the perfect fit for any environment. From church to the battlefield, from work to the couch – no matter the place, you are dressed for the occasion. Have a seat and I'll walk you through this Christian closet.

[10] Finally, my brethren, be strong in the Lord and in the power of His might.[11] Put on the whole armor of God, that you may be able to stand against the wiles of the devil. [12] For we do not wrestle against flesh and blood, but against principalities, against powers, against the rulers of the darkness of this age, against spiritual hosts of wickedness in the heavenly places. [13] Therefore take up the whole armor of God, that you may be able to withstand in the evil day, and having done all, to stand. Ephesians 6:10-13

Did I mention that you're ready for whatever? That includes the fight of your life. Spiritual warfare is real, and it rages on continually. No worries. You're anointed *and* attired! The pieces that God presents by way of His Spirit will thoroughly protect you. *No weapon formed against you shall prosper.* (Isaiah 54:17). This bout can't be fought by wielding razor blades or spewing profanity. Bullets most certainly won't do! Flesh and blood have exited the field. Stuff just got real...and invisible.

[3] For though we walk in the flesh, we do not war according to the flesh. [4] For the weapons of our warfare are not carnal but mighty in God for pulling down strongholds, [5] casting down arguments and every high thing that exalts itself against the knowledge of

God, bringing every thought into captivity to the obedience of Christ. II Corinthians 10:3-5

You are dressed to pull down, cast out, and exercise full authority over the powers of darkness. Your outfit alone equips you to outmatch the enemy. Don't take my word for it; let's examine the wardrobe you're working with.

14 Stand therefore, having girded your waist with truth, having put on the breastplate of righteousness. Ephesians 6:14

I love that belt! Truth centers you well. The functionality is great! How amazing is it that it helps you to *trust in the Lord with all your heart and not lean unto your own understanding?* (Proverbs 3:5). When life attempts to knock you off course, truth is the spiritual gravity that keeps your feet firmly planted. And that breastplate! I would have expected it to be bulky and inconvenient, but no, you *rock* righteousness! Whether you're strolling beside still waters or walking through the valley of the shadow of death, righteousness keeps you rightly positioned in the presence of God.

15 and having shod your feet with the preparation of the gospel of peace. Ephesians 6:15

The good news is these shoes will bless your life! No really, they will. *Blessed are the peacemakers: for they shall be called the children of God.* (Matthew 5:9). These shoes give you status! Yes, these are game changers.

Be honest, have you ever been on a quest to find the perfect shoe? You searched through multiple stores and made sacrifices because the shoes you so desired were worth it. That sole-wear turned heads; this soul-wear transforms lives. *Depart from evil and do good; seek peace and pursue it.* (Psalm 34:14). *If possible, as far as it depends on you, live at peace with everyone.* (Romans 12:18, NLT). Whew! These shoes have a price tag that is paid in the form of integrity. They will cost you humility, rightly seasoned words, and diligence. You know they're worth it. They aren't always the easiest to put on, but they are a perfect fit for the one whose mind stays on Jesus. You *know* they're worth it!

16 above all, taking the shield of faith with which you will be able to quench all the fiery darts of the wicked one. Ephesians 6:16

Your shield is far more durable than any umbrella. As assaults from the evil one rain down on you, faith blocks the attack. It stands between you and all things detrimental. Furthermore, its use goes beyond protection. *Your faith has made you well.* (Matthew 9:22). *And whatever things you ask in prayer, believing, you will receive.* (Matthew 21:22). Faith produces results. Go 'head, *call those things that be not as though they are* according to the Word entrusted to you. (Romans 4:17).

17 And take the helmet of salvation, and the sword of the Spirit, which is the word of God. Ephesians 6:17

Yes! The helmet is your holy hat, which helps you to keep Christ and His saving grace at the forefront of your thoughts. Guard your mind by reflecting on His goodness that rescues you from every low place. *Whatever things are true, whatever things are noble, whatever things are just, whatever things are pure, whatever things are lovely, whatever things are of good report, if there is any virtue and if there is anything praiseworthy—meditate on these things.* (Philippians 4:8).

Last but certainly not least, take up your sword, which is the Word of God. As tightly as you clench the Word you cling to Christ, for Jesus and the Word are one. *And the Word became flesh and dwelt among us, and we beheld His glory, the glory as of the only begotten of the Father, full of grace and truth.* (John 1:14). Hold it securely, because Christ holds you. Wield it in excellence as you follow the Spirit's lead. I know it gets heavy, but the weightiness is for your good. The sword is for your protection and promotion. It is the means by which you *present yourself approved to God, a worker who does not need to be ashamed, rightly dividing the word of truth.* (II Timothy 2:15).

Look in the mirror. There is no shame here. You are your Father's child, fearfully and wonderfully made according to His image. You are the apple of His eye and the reason for His smile. Oh, how He loves to inhabit your praise! You have been called out of darkness into marvelous light. You have been adorned by the Almighty and positioned in a place of power. You *are* a fierce and favored fashionista.

Chapter Seven
Under Siege

Location: Here

Time: Now

Target: You

Uh oh! It is a sobering reality to know that you are the bull's eye. The goal of the enemy is to knock you off course and, if possible, total annihilation. Clearly you are a threat to darkness. The precious treasure within you attracts opposition. Satan has absolute contempt for your godly greatness and will stop at nothing to ensure that your fate is as doomed as his. He is an unrelenting menace, but it is written, *if you faint in the day of adversity, your strength is small.* (Proverbs 24:10). That's not you. Your strength isn't small because Christ is your strength. Stand strong for *when the enemy comes in like a flood, the Spirit of the Lord shall lift up a standard against him. And the Redeemer will come to Zion, and to those who turn from transgression in Jacob, says the Lord.*

(Isaiah 59:9-10). Your Redeemer lives, and so shall you.

No weapon formed against you shall prosper, and every tongue which rises against you in judgment you shall condemn. This is the heritage of the servants of the LORD, and their righteousness is from Me," says the LORD. Isaiah 54:17

12 You shall seek them and not find them—those who contended with you. Those who war against you shall be as nothing, as a nonexistent thing. 13 For I, the LORD your God, will hold your right hand, saying to you, 'Fear not, I will help you. Isaiah 41:12-13

Isaiah is preaching! Do you know Whose you are? El Shaddai, the Lord God Almighty, is your source and strength! He is your fortress and shield. No weapon can overtake you; no lie is damaging enough to break you. The heritage of the servants of the Lord is rich with favor and truth. Your integrity is established in righteousness. Trust that the Lord will continually hold your right hand. He brings you out from under oppressive forces, causing your enemies to become footstools. The dam has broken, oh, but the standard has been raised! Fear not, the Lord is your help.

1 In You, O LORD, I put my trust; let me never be put to shame. 2 Deliver me in Your righteousness, and cause me to escape; incline Your ear to me, and save me. 3 Be my strong refuge, to which I may resort continually; You have given the commandment to save me, for You are my rock and my fortress. ⁴ Deliver me, O my God, out of the hand of the wicked, out of the hand of the unrighteous and cruel man. ⁵ For You are my hope, O Lord GOD; You are my trust from my youth. Psalm 71:1-5

My soul says yes! Lord, I trust You. Lord, I thank You. When all hell breaks loose, You speak and the atmosphere shifts to calmness. Thank You for the power of Your Word. I will speak Your truth. Even when it seems as if all hope is lost, I will offer up sacrifices of praise and trust You all the more. You are worthy, O God!

There is no shame in whole-heartedly trusting the one true and living God. Daughter of the Most High, these attacks won't thwart the move of God in your life. Claim your breakthrough! *⁷ Lift up your heads, O you gates! And be lifted up, you everlasting doors! And the King of glory shall come in. ⁸ Who is this King of glory? The LORD strong and mighty, the LORD mighty in battle!* (Psalm 24:7-8). Father, help Your daughter to know that victory is locked up in her praise. Her worship releases the sweet flow of Your anointing. When her hands go up in surrender, You shall come in. Thank You, Father, for stepping on the scene!

⁷ But we have this treasure in earthen vessels, that the excellence of the power may be of God and not of us. ⁸ We are hard-pressed on every side, yet not crushed; we are perplexed, but not in despair; ⁹ persecuted, but not forsaken; struck down, but not destroyed—¹⁰ always carrying about in the body the dying of the Lord Jesus, that the life of Jesus also may be manifested in our body. ¹¹ For we who live are always delivered to death for Jesus' sake, that the life of Jesus also may be manifested in our mortal flesh. ¹² So then death is working in us, but life in you. II Corinthians 4:7-12

The heat is on. You are under siege, yet unbreakable. Though persecuted, you are not forsaken. No matter how low the valleys you encounter, destruction is not an option. Every time the enemy shows up, it is an opportunity for God to show out on your behalf. Christ is your Way out of trouble and the Truth that illuminates your path. He is the Life that awakens your courage. You are under attack but praise God! Your Savior is undefeated! Victory is yours in the name of Jesus. Release your praise!

Chapter Eight

#PowerFlow

² Behold, God is my salvation; I will trust, and not be afraid: for the LORD JEHOVAH is my strength and my song; He also is become my salvation. ³ Therefore with joy shall ye draw water out of the wells of salvation. Isaiah 12:2-3, KJV

Draw from the well of sweet salvation. Drink deeply for too much of the Lord is never enough. Leave the comforts of shallow faith and venture to new depths. Push past religion and indulge in the intimacy of relationship. The joy of the Lord is your strength so go forward with courage and rejoicing. Do not fear the unknown; instead anticipate the positive possibilities, for in you exists both a well and a river of living water.

The Great I AM touches you in a way that is both personal and interpersonal. He ministers to your personal needs and exceeds that by saturating your life with more than enough of Himself. In doing so, He equips you to minister from the overflow. The well is for you; the river is for others.

⁷ A woman of Samaria came to draw water. Jesus said to her, "Give Me a drink." ⁸ For His disciples had gone away into the city to buy food.

⁹ Then the woman of Samaria said to Him, "How is it that You, being a Jew, ask a drink from me, a Samaritan woman?" For Jews have no dealings with Samaritans.

¹⁰ Jesus answered and said to her, "If you knew the gift of God, and who it is who says to you, 'Give Me a drink,' you would have asked Him, and He would have given you living water."

¹¹ The woman said to Him, "Sir, You have nothing to draw with, and the well is deep. Where then do You get that living water? ¹² Are You greater than our father Jacob, who gave us the well, and drank from it himself, as well as his sons and his livestock?"

¹³ Jesus answered and said to her, "Whoever drinks of this water will thirst again, ¹⁴ but whoever drinks of the water that I shall give him will never thirst. But the water that I shall give him will become in him a fountain of water springing up into everlasting life." John 4:7-14

Fretting the particulars will cause you to overlook the power and prominence of His presence. *You have nothing to draw with, and the well is deep. Are you greater than our father Jacob, who gave us the well?* My dear, this water will quench your thirst for all of eternity. Although Jacob gave you the well, Christ has come that you may have life and have it more abundantly.

Hindsight is 20/20, so it is tempting to scoff at this woman's inability to recognize the greatness that stood before her. Be gracious; all have been guilty of the same. Instead of immediately falling to her knees in worship, she barricaded her heart with skepticism. *Living water? Who does this man think He is?* It is clear that these thoughts crossed her mind. However, Jesus was not only fully aware of His identity but hers as well. He spoke of her sordid past and present, not to shame her but to center her focus on the opportunity before her. *²⁵ The woman said to Him, "I know that the Messiah is coming" (who is called Christ). "When He comes, He will tell us all things." ²⁶ Jesus said to her, "I who speak to you am He."* (John 4:25-26). He *was* telling her all things, but she was missing it. To put an end to the questions, Jesus states, "I am He." I am Christ. I am the Messiah.

The Son can be in your face yet thoughts of the past and present come blind you. Your thirst quencher isn't down the road. It isn't found in a career or a man or a location. It is Christ Jesus, your Savior.

But the water that I shall give will become in [her] a fountain of water springing up into everlasting life. (John 4:14). The well runs deep. It enables you to tap into strength far greater than your own. It sustains you. At times of outward drought, it is your inward provision. The well is your life's constant, never leaving nor forsaking. Sip slowly or gulp greedily; its supply is unending. The well keeps you, comforts you, and replenishes you. The well is the Spirit of God. The well readies you to be a river.

38 He who believes in Me, as the Scripture has said, out of his heart will flow rivers of living water."39 But this He spoke concerning the Spirit, whom those believing in Him would receive; for the Holy Spirit was not yet given, because Jesus was not yet glorified. John 7:38-39

Jesus has been glorified. You have received the Holy Spirit. Flow river flow.

While a well is firmly positioned to give life, a river's movement produces vitality also. A well begins and ends in the same locale, but a river has a journey. A river has a high place of origin, a definite course that runs downhill, contributing water sources, and ends by emptying into a body of water. Stay with me; we're going somewhere.

Life doesn't stop the flow of those who are in Christ. You see, your reason for being – let's call it your place of origin – is one marked with purpose, godly gifts, and distinct talents. You were created for a high life of victory, but trials and temptation threaten to replace mountain top living with low place existing. But God! He *always* provides a way of escape!

Your praying grandmother, discerning teacher, wise pastor, kind neighbor, and far too many others to name have poured into you. They have contributed to building your spirit for such a time as this. With every twist and turn, whether the flow is serene or rapid, yet will you trust Him. You continue to run this course with endurance, because although this path is uniquely yours, there is a larger Body to which you are connected. Every member counts. You count. Every member is important. You are important. Keep flowing. Within you is a well empowering you to be a river if only you will remain planted.

⁷ "Blessed is the [woman] who trusts in the LORD, and whose hope is the LORD. ⁸ For [she] shall be like a tree planted by the waters, which spreads out its roots by the river, and will not fear when heat comes; but its leaf will be green and will not be anxious in the year of drought, nor will cease from yielding fruit. Jeremiah 17:7-8

12 "Most assuredly, I say to you, [she] who believes in Me, the works that I do [she] will do also; and greater works than these [she] will do, because I go to My Father. John 14:12

Stretch out your roots. Go ahead. REACH! Tap into the well of the Spirit of God. Come what may, He will sustain you. In the year of drought, you will continue to bear good fruit. You are destined for great works. Twenty, sixty, a hundredfold – the Living Water flowing through you will cause a harvest of love, joy, peace, and all other spiritual fruit and miracles to flow out of you. Jesus returned to the Father to bestow supernatural power upon you. You have been commissioned to make a difference. The well meets your needs, but the river reaches the multitudes. Flow, river. Flow.

Mentality Shift: **Power**

Chapter Five

The enemy's goal is to trap you in ineffective cycles. In what ways has does he consistently attempt to render you powerless?

Chapter Six

"Faith stands between you and all things detrimental." What are your thoughts on this?

Chapter Seven

What do you see as your greatest challenge to completely surrendering to the Lord?

Chapter Eight

How will fostering an intimate relationship with Christ shift your life?

Mentality Challenge: **Purpose**

Your story has POWER! Reflect on a time when the Lord strengthened you to overcome adversity.

How did you remain in faith throughout the process?

What did you learn about God and yourself as a result of enduring until the end?

PART THREE
Purpose

Esther was taken to King Xerxes at the royal palace in early winter of the seventh year of his reign. ¹⁷ And the king loved Esther more than any of the other young women. He was so delighted with her that he set the royal crown on her head and declared her queen instead of Vashti. Esther 2:16-17, NLT

OK, Esther! Our girl is out here gettin' chosen and what not! She's about to LIVE IT UP in a life of luxury! How beautiful of a happy ending is that? I'm sorry to be the bearer of bad news. Esther being chosen as queen by King Xerxes was not the end; it was just the beginning. Honestly, being chosen is always *just the beginning*. Being called is fabulous... until it's not. I know, I know. Why rain on the royal parade? I love you far too much to leave you in the land of fairy tales and fallacies. There are times when being set apart for God's use feels like a detrimental set up.

The cost of being a daughter of the Almighty is steep. Oh yes, in addition to power and promises are weights to bear and challenges to face. There are rules to learn, opinions to navigate, and responsibilities to carry out. The fun and games of our royal reign get shaken up when purpose comes into play. And hun, purpose is *always* a factor. Let us pause to consider the cost of Esther being set apart before we examine the purpose for her consecration.

12 Before each young woman was taken to the king's bed, she was given the prescribed twelve months of beauty treatments—six months with oil of myrrh, followed by six months with special perfumes and ointments. 13 When it was time for her to go to the king's palace, she was given her choice of whatever clothing or jewelry she wanted to take from the harem. 14 That evening she was taken to the king's private rooms, and the next morning she was brought to the second harem, where the king's wives lived. There she would be under the care of Shaashgaz, the king's eunuch in charge of the concubines. She would never go to the king again unless he had especially enjoyed her and requested her by name. Esther 2:12-14, NLT

The truth is Esther was snatched up as one virgin in a caravan of many virgins. She was primped and primed for 12 months in preparation for the king to have his way with her. Beyond any doubt, every one of the young ladies would lose her virginity to the King Xerxes. The likelihood of ever returning for another rendezvous after that one life-altering night was slim. Our perspective is different because we know the ending was a happy one, but what if it wasn't. Maybe the king would remember Esther's name; maybe he wouldn't. Prior to being crowned, she had no clue what fate would hold. She could be forever forgotten OR she could be relegated to one of his Top 10 concubines, only called up to drop it low and reproduce. Thankfully, neither option was the case, at least not for our girl Esther. The call on her life sanctified her for greatness while also stretching her beyond her comfort zone. Favor isn't fair but neither is it convenient.

13 Mordecai sent this reply to Esther: "Don't think for a moment that because you're in the palace you will escape when all other Jews are killed. 14 If you keep quiet at a time like this, deliverance and relief for the Jews will arise from some other place, but you and your relatives will die. Who knows if perhaps you were made queen for just such a time as this?" Esther 4:13-14, NLT

Make reading the Book of Esther a priority. There are so many twists and turns to our bestie's story that we don't have time to examine right now. Just know that as God is positioning us, the enemy is also coming for us. Esther's "yes" saved an entire nation of people from annihilation. She placed herself in harm's way to prevent multitudes from being slaughtered. Her faith was greater than her fear; the call outweighed the consequences. There was a purpose for Esther's position far beyond what she could have initially known. I can't help but wonder if you have considered why God has chosen you... because He certainly has.

Be not deceived; pain has a way of intertwining itself with purpose. The same God who redeems your soul is well able to redeem your troubles.

Chapter Nine
Speechless
Carmen

God is sooo amazing! Sorry (not sorry). I had to get that praise OUT! You are not reading this by accident. My prayer is that my transparency will spark the release of whatever is keeping you bound so that you can freely live out the purpose of God for your life. The very thought of that might be intimidating. Overcoming that fear is a struggle, but freedom is worth the fight. And trust me, I know what it's like to fight.

The last two months of my life have brought phenomenal life transformation! I rededicated my life to Christ, discovered God's purpose for me, shed some things and people, addressed depression head-on, tapped into joy, and found my voice! That's a lot, I know. In the 5 years prior to this personal revival, I nearly lost my life, had a child out of wedlock, suffered from postpartum depression, got wrongfully terminated from my job, and lost or had my speech impaired on a few occasions. So, when I pause to give God praise, you understand why.

December 2014. The holiday season is supposed to be a time of rejoicing and family gatherings. For me, it's when I came to know God as Healer. I went in for a normal outpatient surgery - correction of a deviated septum and a tonsillectomy. Within 24-hours of being released, I was in the emergency room barely able to walk, speak, or even breathe. It was discovered that I aspirated during surgery, which led to double pneumonia. I was admitted to the hospital the day before my grandmother's funeral. So much for happy holidays...

I remember the look on my great uncle's face when the nurses instructed me to blow into this breathing exercise apparatus. I was supposed to blow hard enough to make the pin move; instead, I began choking uncontrollably. An entire team rushed in like a scene from Grey's Anatomy! And just like that, everything went black. When I woke up, a tube down my throat and my arms were in restraints. Speaking wasn't an option. My family was advised to start preparing for goodbye. In addition to double pneumonia, I developed adult respiratory disruptive syndrome and acute kidney failure. I underwent another surgery and had to receive 6 units of blood. It didn't look good. Thankfully, my family walks by faith and not by sight. I had no voice, so they began to intercede on my behalf.

The road to recovery wasn't an easy one, but eviction day had finally come! No, I wasn't being discharged just yet; instead, the breathing tube was being removed. Do you know how good water was going to taste??? Not to mention being able to talk! My eyes excitedly watched the nurse's every move as she updated my file and put on her gloves. Then, as if enough hadn't already happened, blood began gushing from my nose and mouth! *Lord, really?!?!?* Somehow, someway I was at peace. Honestly, peace was my mood throughout the entire hospital stay. This was around the time that it became apparent that this was bigger than me. Someday I would be able to tell others of God's faithfulness to heal. Looking back, I know God was preparing me for this current season.

But He was wounded for our transgressions, He was bruised for our iniquities; the chastisement for our peace was upon Him, and by His stripes, we are healed. Isaiah 53:3

12 I know how to be abased, and I know how to abound. Everywhere and in all things I have learned both to be full and to be hungry, both to abound and to suffer need. 13 I can do all things through Christ who strengthens me. Philippians 4:12-13

My turnaround didn't come with the restoration of my health. Nope. More was to come. Imagine the weight of an unplanned pregnancy as a pastor's daughter. Uh, yeah. When that pregnancy test read positive, the words that came out of my mouth were NOT, "Thank You, Jesus!" My first concerns were the opinions of my parents and church people. If you grew up in church, you *know* how church people can be! How could I even begin to brace myself for that type of judgment? Despite the stares, I survived.

My son's father is a great individual and an awesome father to our son. Even still, he and I aren't right for each other. Past situations and hurt sent our relationship into a downward spiral from which we were never able to recover. It was partly me. Due to a combination of being displeased with my post-pregnancy body and fear of having another child without being married, I refused to have sex with him. Guilt played a role as well. I knew better! My parents instilled biblical principles in me! I felt as though I failed them and God.

Instead of expressing these concerns to my then-boyfriend, I shut down. God was never a topic of discussion with us, so I was unsure of where he stood spiritually. I went to church every Sunday; he did not. Remaining silent seemed easier when it came to conversations about God. Like the ol' folks used to say, we were unevenly yoked. Things that bothered me spiritually didn't bother him. Instead of uplifting him and encouraging him to develop a closer relationship with God, I began to slack. I stopped going to church and my prayer life became almost nonexistent. Life began to revolve around him and our son. There was nothing to give; my well was dry. Break up. Make up. Repeat the cycle. Discomfort became a normal way of life. A year of this led me to my breaking point.

Frequent headaches were not the norm for me, but here I was having them. One particular day during a professional development session at work, I attempted to speak and immediately knew something was wrong. This wasn't my first time not being able to speak. Previously, some type of trauma was to blame. Nothing was going on at this time. This should not have been happening! I went to the bathroom to call my mom. I was stuttering uncontrollably. Tests, tests, and more tests. You name it, the doctors looked for it. All clear. They attributed the temporary speech impediment to migraines. I was back to normal within a week.

November 3, 2019. This one afternoon brought revelation and a shift in mindset. Let's rewind first. I met this one girl at a networking event a few weeks prior. God knows what we need even when we don't. I reached out in need of clarity regarding my side business and ended up getting so much more. We talked as if we had known each other for years! Thereafter, she began sending "random" text messages that were nowhere near random. They always spoke to exactly what I was going through even though she didn't know me personally. When she invited me to a kickback at her house I accepted without knowing what to expect. *I wonder if we finna turn up, play some games, or do crafts?* None of the above. Not for a second did I think we would be a group of women talking about God! Imagine it: a young adult hosting a gathering to talk about Jesus. Now, *that* is definitely uncommon these days! Before it ended, I had the opportunity to share my testimony. When I finished, the host asked if I had ever considered speaking or writing a book. She went on to say that it seems like my voice is attacked every time I get sick. I was blown away. One, I never shared my desire to speak and write with anyone. Two, her question brought the understanding and confirmation I needed regarding the loss of speech.

That day sparked a revival in my soul. The host continues to pour into me and walk out this faith journey with me. Faith run might be more accurate because no time is being wasted. God began revealing His promises for me within days of the kickback. I started meeting with a therapist to declutter my life. I was excited to dive into the Word again. Life was amazing... but it wasn't peachy.

Part of my life renewal process was ending the relationship with my child's father. He had to move out. Our arrangement wasn't going to work. I came to the realization that I couldn't love him because I didn't love myself. Ouch. I gave so much of me over the years without taking time to replenish that I finally hit rock bottom. We had to part ways in order for my focus to realign. God told me enough was enough! I have come to learn that seasons change with time but cycles change with me. Imagine a hamster on a wheel. He will forever go around and around until he chooses to change. I can say all day, "I'm going to lose 10 pounds," but if I never make changes, I will never see results. Once the cycle ended I could see and hear more clearly. I drew near to God and He drew near to me.

Move your heart closer and closer to God, and he will come even closer to you. But make sure you cleanse your life, you sinners, and keep your heart pure and stop doubting. James 4:8, TPT

To those reading this, know that the cycle changes with you. Identify your cycle, get off the wheel and change your direction.

About Carmen Carmen is a Nashville native who enjoys all things creative! She holds a Bachelor's degree in Communications from the University of Tennessee at Chattanooga and a Master's degree in Elementary Education from Tennessee State University. When she isn't in the classroom or spending time with her charming son, RJ, Carmen's attention is turned to discovering and living out the call of God on her life.

Connect

Instagram: @carmenmstephens

Chapter Ten
Redefined
ShaRonda

Listen. I grew up in the church! God was introduced to me early in life, and you know the lasting effects of first impressions. The Lord God Almighty was presented to me as this Man on a throne who unleashed His wrath on all who didn't live right. I was into adulthood and far from my strict upbringing before realizing I had been miseducated. As "churchy" people would say, I fell from grace. Grace. Aside from being one-half of the twins - when you hear mercy, you hear grace - I had no personal revelation of what it meant. It was not until it was extended to me that I came to understand grace and recognize my need for it. The Father's love for me was revealed through His people during my lowest and darkest times.

To say that I was depressed is an understatement. I hid it well, or so I thought. The Holy Spirit has a way of giving people discernment to see beyond the surface. *My grace is sufficient and nothing you do will make Me leave you.* Over and over again, God kept affirming His faithfulness to never leave nor forsake me. Although I recognized His voice, it was not in sync with the character of the judgmental Man introduced to me as a child. He sounded... loving and compassionate and even patient. It took fighting for my life for me to understand what God was saying. While on my deathbed I heard Him say, "There is still work for you to do, and you will not leave this earth with your work undone." Confirmation came. A group of college friends visited me in the hospital and echoed the same instruction God has spoken time and time again: LEAVE!

Leave that toxic relationship and come back to Me
so that I can activate what I placed inside of you.

According to I Samuel 15:22, "Obedience is better than sacrifice." So much of my time, energy, and livelihood had already been sacrificed to no benefit of my own. Surely obedience had to be the better way. I walked away from my boyfriend of 5 years. Leaving everything behind, I moved in with my parents at the age of 31. Back to square one. Loss of material possessions is one thing, but I returned to my childhood home with a lack of physical *and* spiritual strength. That's a totally different mountain to climb! I cried for weeks due to having to rely on my mother and father. It wasn't supposed to be this way! I have always been self-sufficient, which is probably why I needed to learn that HIS grace is sufficient.

I have forgiven you; now, forgive yourself.

Did you know that trauma has residue? My residue went back further than my relationship. It started before my fall. There were layers upon layers of wrong teaching, misunderstanding, and misalignment. This isn't finger-pointing or me refusing to take responsibility for my actions. I owned my wrongs, so much so that they defined me for a period of time. The Lord reassured me that redefinition was in process. I had to lose control for Him to gain control. Simply put, I had to allow Him to reign from the throne of my heart.

I am not a victim or a fallen saint. I am a daughter of the Great I AM! His favor, which has always rested on my life, is rising up in ways that are causing my faith to be stretched beyond its borders. For years, others have spoken of how His gifts and anointing rest on my life; I see clearly now that His hand has been on me from the start. As religion and tradition fall away, authentic relationship shifts to the forefront. Churchiness convinced me to be humble, sit down... play the background. The Lord is saying not so! Well, be humble, yes. Sit down and fall back, no. It's more like, "Arise and shine; for your light has come!" (Isaiah 60:1)

I am in the process of redevelopment. I am lost... but in a good way, a godly way. I am engulfed in true identity; I abide fully in the presence of the King. His Spirit lives in me and rests on me; He governs my steps. As instructed, I laid to rest the old me and find myself daily stepping more deeply into who He has called me to be. I am destined to be a curse breaker in this generation. My freedom is not just for me; it's for the masses. Like my Daddy, one word or phrase is not enough to define me.

I AM NEW

Therefore if any man be in Christ, he is a new creature: old things are passed away; behold, all things are become new. II Corinthians 5:17

All things new! I am no longer who I was but who God has called me to be!

I AM CHOSEN

But ye are a chosen generation, a royal priesthood, a holy nation, a peculiar people; that ye should shew forth the praises of him who hath called you out of darkness into his marvellous light. I Peter 2:9, KJV

God chose me from the beginning. I am *His* daughter. I am royalty and will continue to shine bright because I have been called into His marvelous light!

I AM BOLD

For this reason I remind you to fan into flame the gift of God, which is in you through the laying on of my hands. For the Spirit God gave us does not make us timid, but gives us power, love and self-discipline. II Timothy 1:6-7, NIV

Remember, I am a curse breaker. Curses cannot be broken without boldness. I will not back down from the call!

I AM ENOUGH

You are of God, little children, and have overcome them, because He who is in you is greater than he who is in the world. I John 4:4

In the past, others believed in me more than I believed in myself. Many of my accomplishments are the result of trying to prove myself. This new territory - the land of purpose and promise that I am called to - is filled with souls that the Lord has qualified and positioned me to serve. He didn't cause my fall or past pains and still, He lovingly causes all of it to work together for His good. (Romans 8:28). Surely, His grace is sufficient. Now, I can boldly proclaim that I believe in me because He lives in me!

About ShaRonda

Overcoming power is mixed into even the messiest story when the narrative and its outcome are surrendered to the Lord. Through Share Your Story, a ministry founded on the truth of Revelation 12:11, ShaRonda strives to strengthen souls through the power of God's ability to redeem any story. ShaRonda is most passionate about serving others and advancing the Kingdom of God.

Connect

Instagram: @sharondafreeman

Chapter Eleven
Pivots, Pain, & Purpose
Tina

Pivotal moments. We all have them. Some are so positive that we have no doubt they were placed along our paths to drive us toward purpose. Other moments, although no less life-defining, come into our lives for reasons not ordained by God. As an adult, I recognize what that negative pivotal moment was for me. It has taken many years to sort it all out in my mind.

pivotal moment - a duration of time possessing crucial importance in relation to the development or success of an individual

I was molested by a teenage boy at the age of ten. I never told my parents or anyone else for that matter. Rather than allowing them to be burdened by guilt and shame over the situation, I chose to carry it. My childhood reasoning skills led me to believe that if I allowed it to happen I should at least be responsible enough to bear the weight of the negative emotions that followed. *This is nothing compared to what others endure!* That's what I told myself. Mentally downplaying what happened to me physically was supposed to make me feel better. It didn't. Isn't it strange how we take on guilt and shame for things we didn't invite or cause? I look back and wonder how life would have been different if this one pivotal moment had never occurred...

Would I have stayed on the right track?

What better choices might I have made?

Where did all of these new fears originate?

I was brought up in a good home with wonderful parents. This sudden surge of fear didn't make sense. Now, *everything* frightened me! The unexplainable fear eventually led to self-destruction. Partying, promiscuity, binge eating, and putting God on the backburner - my identity in Christ became buried under toxic coping mechanisms. Any confidence that I ever had in Whose I was or what I was called to do was lost behind the masks. You know the masks. We put our best faces forward, even if that means presenting a fake face. I hid my behavior well. I completed high school, earned a master's degree, got married, had children, and worked in my chosen career. My children were raised in church just as I was raised in church.

The Church. I grew up in the Methodist Church where I was taught the basics of God's Word and His love for me. No matter what was happening in life, my mother always (and I mean ALWAYS) made sure we attended church. Even throughout my rebellious stage, she lovingly ushered me into the house of the Lord.

I knew God loved me. My heart has always been tender toward the Lord. Still, part of me struggled to reconcile the God who gave His Son for me and filled His Word with promises for me with the God who allowed such an atrocity to happen to me. I thought I was His daughter! I went through the motions and did what was expected of me. I moved through life with shame and unexplainable fear tagging along.

Oh, this incredible fear! Fear of not being in control, fear of failure, fear of not being accepted, fear of loss, fear of not being enough, fear of letting my children out of my sight, fears from the past bubbling up in the present - it was unending! I felt as though I would never do or be enough to rid myself of the guilt, shame, and fear that latched onto me at ten years old. But God! Have you experienced coming to a familiar passage of Scripture - as in you have encountered it hundreds of times - and then BAM, you get hit with new meaning and new revelation? Exactly! That's what happened! The words penetrated my soul as if written specifically for me.

6 Therefore I remind you to stir up the gift of God which is in you through the laying on of my hands. 7 For God has not given us a spirit of fear, but of power and of love and of a sound mind. II Timothy 1:6-7

WOW! God knew me from my mother's womb! He had a plan in mind when forming me in darkness. (Psalm 139:13-14). He knew I would face adversity and pain; He knew my decisions wouldn't always be godly. He also knew what He placed in my spirit. The Father gave me the strength and courage needed to recover from the past and reclaim my identity in Him. There was a choice to make. Would I cling to false identities and insecurities and risk passing them from generation to generation or would I stand firm in my Christ-identity? I chose the latter so that others would know of Christ's grace and redemptive power. Hallelujah!

Sin alters the plan God has for us, but it does not cancel it.

Pastor Eric Kelleher

Bridge of Hope Church

Being molested was no more a part of God's plan for my life than the destructive behavior in which I once chose to engage. Despite what the enemy has told you, negative pivotal moments were not the Lord's will for you. Something happening or even being allowed does not mean it was ordained. By God's Word and His Holy Spirit, we become empowered to survive our altered courses and transform into vessels of honor for His glory. The hardships that you and I have endured do not exempt us from being used, blessed, or loved by God. Pivotal moments don't get to steal our princess status!

I can do all things through Christ who strengthens me.
Philippians 4:13

Today, I stand boldly knowing WHOSE I am. I am married to a wonderful man who experienced deliverance from drug addiction and the horrific lifestyle that it entails. He and I have been together for 29 years; we divorced and remarried twice but that's another story! He has blessed me with 2 handsome sons and a beautiful stepdaughter. I tease him that if it not for him, I wouldn't know how to teach others how to overcome adversity. Truthfully, it is the victory seen in my personal life, his life, and our marriage that strengthens my faith to keep believing for the things I cannot see. I continue to seek and petition God for revelation in the battles our children currently face. God's promises and His timeliness will be just as faithful to our children as to us.

My intentions were not to bear my soul as I have and yet, here we are. God had a plan that exceeded my comfort zone. My prayer is that you will be encouraged to always keep the Lord rightly positioned as the head of your life and trust in His timing. Be strong in the Lord and the power of His might. (Ephesians 6:10).

But those who wait on the Lord shall renew their strength; they shall mount up with wings like eagles, they shall run and not be weary, they shall walk and not faint. Isaiah 40:31

About Tina   Tina is a Methodist-raised, Pentecostal girl who knows firsthand the power of God and the Baptism of His Holy Spirit! She shares her story in hopes that other women will recognize their identity in Christ and become empowered to overcome life's pivotal moments. Tina is a wife, mother, and grandmother of one. Most importantly, she is a lover of Jesus.

Instagram: @tinalvine

Chapter Twelve
Finally Bold
Ariel

Ugh! Why me? Being unique is great unless you're a six-year-old little girl who wants nothing more than to fit in. It was clear to me that I was different but I couldn't quite put my finger on how or why. I just knew that something was blocking me from being like everyone else. Prophetic words of things to come were spoken over my life at an early age. That was cute and all, but what about now?!?!? At that present moment, blending in sounded so much more appealing. I tried. Man, did I try! Personality after personality was piled on in an attempt to find me - the version of Ariel that could be received and loved by all. Oh, the innocent wishes that childhood brings!

It wasn't until after high school graduation that the scales began to fall from my eyes. "Began" indicates a process. It definitely wasn't an overnight revelation. As divine downloads worked their way into my heart from the Father's mouth, my identity in Christ began to be revealed. I was starting to become comfortable in my own skin. Then, doubt surfaced. What if the *real* me wasn't enough? How would living for God affect my life... or limit my fun... or prevent me from living on *my* terms? Instead of courageously stepping into the unknown hope and future ordained for me, I went to work creating the life that I thought was best. God wasn't forgotten. Oh no! I gave Him time every Wednesday night, Sunday morning, and called on Him in cases of emergency. Judge not lest ye be judged! I'm not the only one who has been guilty of putting Him in a box.

Want to know the funny thing about trying to contain God? IT'S IMPOSSIBLE! He doesn't stay tucked away well at all! Every time I went down the wrong path, the Holy Spirit would check me. The need to be in control kept rising up and I kept right on doing what I wanted to do. Well, sort of. The reality is people-pleasing dictated my life. I had to be everything I was expected to be - dress a certain way, act a certain way, and have a certain group of friends. If all the criteria weren't meant, my mind told me I wasn't enough. That's the pressure of the world, especially as brought to us by social media, right? But that still, small voice never stopped speaking. The Lord my God had a plan for me.

During freshman year of college, I found myself 6 hours away from home. Riding my parents' spiritual coattails wasn't an option. I drew closer to God out of desire rather than a result of being forced. Nearness leads to transparency and transparency doesn't exist without vulnerability. Maybe not for you but for me, vulnerability feels like weakness. The solution? Insert distance. One by one, I began chipping away at people and things. They weren't bad people. In my mind, I was the bad person. The best friends/brothers/sisters that made up my circle of friends throughout my teens didn't know the true me. They knew the Ariel I presented to them. These people had no knowledge of who I was at home or the depression I battled or how I felt about the things they said behind my back. They only knew what they were allowed to know: my people-pleasing performance. Parting ways was easier. I believed they wouldn't know how to love me through my flaws. Certainly, they wouldn't know how to receive this strong, loving, lioness of God that was rising up. I didn't even know how to love myself in the midst of these dueling realities.

Joining an on-campus Bible study helped strengthen my walk with Christ. Have you experienced the stretching that takes place when you lean into God? That's what was happening. I felt great! As I gained an understanding of my Christ-identity, the enemy popped up to challenge it. He used my past against me and made me feel unworthy of God's promises. As much as we seek to study God's Word and learn His ways, the devil studies us too. He watches how we move and makes note of our weaknesses. He knew feelings of inadequacy were a stumbling block for me. Do you think he didn't try to trip me every chance he got??? God began revealing my calling in 2009. My determination to make it happen - to be found "enough" for the mantle - caused the process to be more difficult than necessary. My parents were hard workers. Drive and determination were in my DNA. Be still and know that He is God? Nah. I got this. And just like that, my timing went to war with God's timing.

For I know the thoughts that I think toward you, says the Lord, thoughts of peace and not of evil, to give you a future and a hope. Jeremiah 29:11

It was never my responsibility to *make* God's will happen, but I was for sure going to try. Who knew that the key to walking in purpose is surrender? I spent YEARS wondering why *my* life had to be so hard. Why weren't *my* prayers being answered? *God, why aren't the promises YOU spoke over me manifesting in my life?!?!* Broken. Angry. Frustrated. And standing in my own way. The Father's timing is crucial; it's how He protects us from ourselves.

Going in circles became tiresome. *How? Why? When?* Questioning everything was unfruitful. When I came to the end of me, God was right there. He received me like a patient Daddy. When I collapsed into the comfort of authentic intimacy, the boldness needed to be the true me was unlocked. Rather than forcing an identity, I submitted to who God says I am. If this sounds as easy as a split decision, I assure you it was NOT! *I don't want this! I don't want this! I don't want this!* The fight was real. I went back and forth so many times, so afraid of what the call would cost me. The wiser thing is to consider how much running and striving and people-pleasing had cost.

If you are in that season of running, stop. Breathe. Consider from Whom you are running. True enough, submitting to the will of God doesn't always feel good. We have to die to ourselves, pick up our cross, and follow Christ. But when I tell you it's worth it, it is. It *really* is. God is doing something in and through you that is bigger than your fears and sure to stretch your faith. He is positioning you for things that are exceedingly and abundantly beyond what you could ever ask or imagine... for His glory. I know because that's what He's doing for me. And I know He loves you no less.

Create in me a clean heart, O God, And renew a right and steadfast spirit within me. Psalms 51:10, AMP

In 2018, exactly 9 years after God told me who I was, I began to learn more about who He is. I learned that others are not my God. Neither my husband nor my parents could be what He is to me. My friends couldn't fill that role either. I said, "YES," and an unimaginable, unexplainable process was initiated. The pressure increased; the heat was on! My husband and I experienced our fifth miscarriage. *Waaaiiittt! Lord, I said yes! I surrendered!* This time was different. IT. BROKE. ME. Feelings of "less than" came rushing back. Depression returned with a vengeance. Isolation became my uncomfortable comfort. Some days getting out of bed was impossible. I didn't want to bathe or see the light. After about a week, I forced myself to become functional.

There was a moment in my life

when I couldn't tell the difference

between a window and a mirror.

I could look into both

and see everything but myself.

Windows & Mirrors by Rudy Francisco

Here is the issue: We were never created to just function. No matter how hard or dark of a season we find ourselves in, it doesn't define us. We have to keep walking to reach victory. Valleys are not our forever homes, although they can feel unending. The Lord uprooted me from the comfort of my apartment, inserted space between my "framily" and me, and called me to step away from mentoring teens for a season. He sent me to my hometown - the place I loved to visit but never wanted to live - while my husband was deployed. At times, it is necessary to return to the place where we were first established. Admittedly, I allowed myself to become so wrapped up in titles and accomplishments that the Lord had to remind me of who He called me to be from the very start. Of course, the devil tried to shame me. I was so embarrassed by my mental state that I disconnected from everything and everyone without warning. The sense of embarrassment increased, but I had no choice but to work through it. *If breaking is necessary, then please, Lord, let me break well...*

Every day became intentional. I learned that both good and bad times work together to mold me into the true me. As much as it sucks to admit it, the heartache, discomfort, and frustration were no less significant than my wins. All of these factors led me to the boldness of my roar.

The wicked flee when no one pursues them, but the righteous are as bold as a lion. Proverbs 28:1 AMP

The boldness in me speaks to the boldness in you: BE BOLD! I struggled to articulate this message, but that doesn't mean I don't have a message. It is in the jumbled mess of life's ups and downs that God molds, shapes, and makes us. I am who God says I am! The purpose and passion He placed within me are enough for me to empower you, so repeat after me...

I AM ENOUGH.

About Ariel   Ariel is a lioness of God who has found her roar! She is impassioned by the desire to help other women realize and live out their full potential in Christ. After spending years wrestling with her God-ordained calling, she now stands confidently in her identity as a woman of God, discerner of His voice, and mouthpiece for His message. Several miscarriages and a season of spiritual pregnancy led to the rediscovery of her true self. Now, Ariel lives to tell ladies near and far, "YOU ARE ENOUGH!" This journey of self-awareness wrapped in intimacy with God has placed a demand on her uniqueness while requiring nothing less than BOLD FAITH. Through divine labor pains, Ariel has birthed her purpose.

Instagram: @BoldFaithOutreach

Website: www.BoldFaithOutreach.com

Mentality Shift: **Purpose**

It is written, "And they have defeated him by the blood of the Lamb and by their testimony. And they did not love their lives so much that they were afraid to die." (Revelation 12:11, NLT) Begin overcoming by writing your story.

Keep writing...

I'm sure there's more...

Release precedes your reign. The Lord is redeeming your story.

Mentality Challenge: **Promise**

How would life change if you consistently lived with an accurate revelation of God's love for you?

Christ gave His life for you. How does this fact resonate with you?

"God isn't holding you back; He's building you up." Be honest; in what ways do you feel as though faith and obedience are hindering you?

PART FOUR

Promise

Fact: *The Lord God is a sun and shield: the Lord will give grace and glory; no good thing will He withhold from them who walk uprightly.* Psalm 84:11

Think about the magnitude of this verse: *For God so loved the world that He gave His only begotten Son, that whoever believes in Him should not perish but have everlasting life.* (John 3:16). God the Father, your Heavenly Father, sent Jesus, God the Son, to earth for the sole purpose of dying for the atonement of humanity's sins. Shall we personalize it? My sin. Your sin. You were worth the Blood of Jesus. Yes, you. *For when we were still without strength, in due time Christ died for the ungodly.* (Romans 5:6). Even without being worthy, you were worth it.

⁶ Who, being in the form of God, did not consider it robbery to be equal with God, ⁷ but made Himself of no reputation, taking the form of a bondservant, and coming in the likeness of men. ⁸ And being found in appearance as a man, He humbled Himself and became obedient to the point of death, even the death of the cross. Philippians 2:6-8

At times, returning to the basics is necessary. Remaining anchored to the hope of your salvation is vital to continuing this journey of faith, freedom, and steadfastness. We cannot become desensitized to the truth on which we stand, because that truth is the reality of what Christ has done, is doing, and will do in our lives. This truth – the fact that you/me/we are worth it – is the purpose for our being and the source of our strength.

We must remember that in the eyes of Jesus, we are worth it. If He had to do it again, He would. But praise God, He doesn't have to! His work was completed on the Cross. Death lost its sting, and the grave lost its victory. As the end draws near and we progress from glory to glory, there is comfort in knowing we win.

As Blood-bought sacrifices, we have the privilege of partaking in the unfolding of the greatest love story ever told. You, my friend, are far from an envious onlooker. This is nothing like those solo, chick-flick movie nights that leave you longing for intimacy on another level. However, this *is* intimacy on another level. This experience is pure and real and life-changing. There is no perversion or guilt. This moves you and gives life. Too much is never enough because exceeding abundance has been promised. This is nothing like those lonely nights. No ma'am – far from it! It's rated G for godly, and you're right in the middle of the action.

You are worth it. Make that a foundational truth for your faith. Piercing stares from others don't change that. A past riddled with rejection doesn't change that. Sin? Hun-ney, let me tell you, *where sin abounds, grace abounds much more.* (Romans 5:20). Of course, that's not a license to sin, but it's surely security for our imperfections. You aren't perfect; neither is God asking you to be. He simply wants you to understand and live like you're worth it.

I DARE you to believe that God loves you. Wait! Don't flippantly dismiss this challenge as elementary. *Oh yeah, I know He loves me.* Do you really? When you *really* receive revelation of God's love, your life is revolutionized; it literally takes on new meaning. There is nothing ordinary about waking up to a new day; for you understand that each day is filled with purpose and His presence. The reality of His inconceivable love reaches the depths of your soul, intertwining with your heart to the extent that each beat echoes a zeal for His will.

When you really come face-to-face with God's love and understand that He deems you *worthy* of receiving His love, surrendering your all becomes an honor. There is no greater fulfillment than that found in serving Him.

Knowing that you're worth it causes you to develop distaste for disobedience and a hunger for righteousness. Saying adios to the old you is doable because the new you knows Love and Life and Light. The new you knows you were created with purpose in mind, and that purpose has promises and provision attached to it. Dismiss the misconceptions. God isn't holding you back; He's building you up.

He is the Father, who clothes you in grace and glory. Daughter of the Most High, no good thing shall be withheld from you. He is the Daddy that affirms. His is the Voice that calls you by name. He is the Sanctifier who cleanses you and the Faithful One who shall return for you...because He loves you...and you're worth it.

Chapter Thirteen
Affirmative Action

Relax. It's not what you think. This is not a dedication to girl power, equality, or contemporary social agendas – some of which have their appropriate time and place, none of which will be our topic of focus. Clear your mind of preconceived notions regarding affirmative action because this is the spiritual twist.

Therefore being justified by faith, we have peace with God through our Lord Jesus Christ. Romans 5:1

Pause. You are confirmed in Christ – established, deeply rooted, and complete in your Savior. Let that digest and we'll move on.

Ready? Let's continue.

Simply put, justified is to be made right. By faith, you are right and acceptable in the eyes of God and now have access to true intimacy with Him by Christ. From this divine connection comes a peace that surpasses all understanding and strength-producing joy. What I am telling you is that *this* affirmative action opens the door for you to do life on another level.

For it is written, *"Through whom also we have access by faith into this grace in which we stand, and rejoice in hope of the glory of God."* (Romans 5:2). Understand that life nor death, height nor depth can separate you from the life-sustaining and overflow-creating force that is God's love as is promised according to Romans 8:38-39. These are more than mere words. This is a declaration of truth. Rest assured that Love (for God is love) is with you.

The Holy Spirit, who dwells in you, is accompanied by the grace of God, which covers you. Grace empowers you. It pushes back limitations as it amplifies self-control. What's the correlation you ask? Grace enlarges your territory, at the same time ensuring that you have the character and discipline needed to operate at a new level of blessing and responsibility. Yes, with new dimensions come new duties.

3 And not only that, but we also glory in tribulations, knowing that tribulation produces perseverance; 4 and perseverance, character; and character, hope. 5 Now hope does not disappoint, because the love of God has been poured out in our hearts by the Holy Spirit who was given to us. Romans 5:3-5

You are justified, but life doesn't stop happening. Trials will come. Stand and see the saving grace of God. Through every hardship, the prospect of persevering is made available. Perseverance develops your character according to that of Christ. This is the reality that fuels your hope: He who endured all things for your sake intercedes on your behalf to the Father.

Abba Father, help your daughter to see the light in the midst of darkness. Grant her serenity in the midst of confusion. Remind her that the schemes of the enemy will not prevail against her. Send the Comforter to soothe her. It's okay that she weeps tonight; morning will bring her great joy.

When bad is all you see, know that better is coming. Let not your heart be troubled for the hope you have in your heavenly Father will not lead to disappointment. His loving presence fills you, equipping you to stand strong even in the center of calamity. Hard times have an expiration date. Rest assured that your mourning will be turned into dancing for His name's sake.

You are approved by God. You aren't perfect, but you are no less precious in His sight. God looks to you and smiles. At the point of salvation, He affirmed your position as His child by wiping the slate clean, giving you a new heart, and pronouncing you a new person.

26A new heart also will I give you, and a new spirit will I put within you: and I will take away the stony heart out of your flesh, and I will give you a heart of flesh. 27And I will put My Spirit within you, and cause you to walk in My statutes, and you shall keep My judgments and do them. Ezekiel 36:26-27, KJV

This means that anyone who belongs to Christ has become a new person. The old life is gone; a new life has begun! II Corinthians 5:17, NLT

God said it; that settles it, so you may as well accept it. Have faith! You are blessed and highly favored. The most radical affirmative action is being granted the privilege of being born again. Receive this prayer and know that you are affirmed by your Father:

24 The LORD bless you and keep you; 25 the LORD make His face shine upon you, and be gracious to you; 26 the LORD lift up His countenance upon you, and give you peace. Numbers 6:24-26

Chapter Fourteen
Image is EVERYTHING

Here's a difficult question: Who are you minus the identifying roles? Let me explain. If not a mother, sister, friend, daughter, or wife then who are you? That's tough. What I am asking is who are you at the core? Even in your most simplified state, you are *still* someone of significance. You are still preciously valuable. Who is this person of worth? What happens when you aren't sure how to answer the question?

Experiences shape you. Life threatens to break you. When placed in new situations, your personality makes its debut. But who are you?

Your doctorate degree is proudly displayed, but who are you? Long sleeves cover the scars of a cutter's past, but who are you? You have an immaculate home, well-behaved children, and a husband who adores you...BUT WHO ARE *YOU*? Who does that husband love? Whose past, marred with pain and self-hatred, has been covered by the Blood? Who is the lady behind the accolades? Really, dear princess, who *are* you?

These questions aren't meant to be condescending. This isn't an argument. You *are* somebody. With or without a list of accomplishments, you have worth. Even with baggage, you have value. However, if image is everything, it is necessary to comprehend the root of who you are so that the proper image is reflected.

Let's delve into the definitive qualities of your uniqueness. You are amazing! Embrace that truth. Acceptance comes by understanding. In discovering the root of your awesomeness you'll be persuaded that you are, indeed, AMAZING!

And God said, Let Us make man in Our image, after Our likeness: and let them have dominion over the fish of the sea, and over the fowl of the air, and over the cattle, and over all the earth, and over every creeping thing that creeps upon the earth. So God created man in His Own image, in the image of God created He him; male and female created He them. Genesis 1:26-27

I hope your shouting shoes are laced tight! You are made in the image of God! If you were never anything more than His daughter, that would be MORE than enough. Being positioned as the King's offspring, empowered by His grace, and blessed with His promises makes you MORE THAN ENOUGH! You aren't lacking. You are not inadequate. In Christ, you are more than enough. Receive that.

God, the Father – ruler of all, majestic and just, sovereign and gracious, all-seeing yet forgiving. God, the Son – meek yet powerful, the Word wrapped in flesh, Lord and Friend, our victory. God, the Holy Spirit – comforter, teacher, counselor, and guide.

This is nowhere near an exhaustive list of who God is. The point is this, the one true and living God knew you before time began. He formed you in the womb and gave you a name. He washed you in His Blood and filled you with His Spirit. He formed you in His image and designed a path for you. God opens doors that no man can shut and positions you under heaven's outpour. It is crucial that you realize how special you are because the father of lies contrives schemes to trick you into cuddling dysfunction.

¹ Now the serpent was more cunning than any beast of the field which the LORD God had made. And he said to the woman, "Has God indeed said, 'You shall not eat of every tree of the garden'?"
² And the woman said to the serpent, "We may eat the fruit of the trees of the garden; ³ but of the fruit of the tree which is in the midst of the garden, God has said, 'You shall not eat it, nor shall you touch it, lest you die.'" ⁴ Then the serpent said to the woman, "You will not surely die. ⁵ For God knows that in the day you eat of it your eyes will be opened, and you will be like God, knowing good and evil." Genesis 3:1-5

Your eyes will be opened and you will be like God. If truth sets us free then surely lies are binding. That which you stand for and on is the foundation of who you are. Adam and Eve were made in God's image – clothed in righteousness and truth. They roamed freely, joyfully, and peacefully in God's garden of perfect provision. Wholeness was all they knew because it is all God had blessed them to know. What gain does a realization of evil bring?

16 To the woman He said: "I will greatly multiply your sorrow and your conception; in pain you shall bring forth children; your desire shall be for your husband, and he shall rule over you." 17 Then to Adam He said, "Because you have heeded the voice of your wife, and have eaten from the tree of which I commanded you, saying, 'You shall not eat of it': "Cursed is the ground for your sake; in toil you shall eat of it all the days of your life. 18 Both thorns and thistles it shall bring forth for you, and you shall eat the herb of the field. 19 In the sweat of your face you shall eat bread till you return to the ground, for out of it you were taken; for dust you are, and to dust you shall return." Genesis 3:16-19

There is nothing new under the sun. The enemy continues to attack our thoughts by 1) Convincing us that we are less than God created us to be and 2) Causing us to believe God is withholding something that would add to our quality of life. The *only* thing being withheld from Adam and Eve was the curse and its implications. An understanding of evil granted them nothing worth having and cost them that which exceeds any price. The fall created distance between them and God.

In the name of Jesus, I declare that you WILL know who you are!

⁴Coming to Him as to a living stone, rejected indeed by men, but chosen by God and precious, ⁵you also, as living stones, are being built up a spiritual house, a holy priesthood, to offer up spiritual sacrifices acceptable to God through Jesus Christ. I Peter 2:4-5

This relationship is progressive; it keeps getting better. My sister, this journey is one from glory to glory. Did you miss the fact that you *are* a living stone, shaped in the image of the Living Stone? You *are* being built up as a spiritual house, a holy priesthood. These proclamations are present tense. You are positioned to enter the holy of holies. You have access to the throne room of God.

Therefore, it is also contained in the Scripture, "Behold, I lay in Zion a Chief Cornerstone, elect, precious, and [she] who believes on Him will by no means be put to shame." I Peter 2:6

Do not be intimidated by the weightiness of the call to be identified as His. Rather relish in the fact that you are called and accepted. When God formed you, He knew you wouldn't maneuver through life flawlessly. Neither was that the expectation. The Blood covers your mishaps and stumbles. In times past, the enemy has succeeded in convincing you to operate in lower-level thinking. That ends now! Shake off the shame! *For godly sorrow produces repentance leading to salvation, not to be regretted; but the sorrow of the world produces death.* (II Corinthians 7:10). You are on the winning team! No need to hang your head low; the past is no more, and your future blazes brightly because Christ has gone before you to prepare the way.

Having a revelation of God's love for you gives the enemy pause. It gets him out of your ear and back under your feet. It is imperative that you move beyond rote clichés and become fully persuaded enough to proclaim that, "Yes, Jesus loves me!" Go ahead, I'll wait.

Boo, at the core you are chosen! Without taking any natural roles into account, you are free! Your most simplified state is still stupendous because you *are* the righteousness of God by Christ Jesus! Can I get an amen?

Sin is pleasurable for a season but, my dear, it's time to come up from short-term thinking. A sweetly whispered, momentary lie is no match for God's timeless promises. The Father is in this with you for the long haul; He has sent His Spirit to walk it out with you. What shall it be – temporary thrills or tenaciously thriving? Choose the latter and make room for the real you to shine.

You see, image is everything and you have been hand-crafted for greatness by the Awesome Wonder. Amazingness is ingrained in your divine DNA. You were formed with eternity in mind so think beyond today. Before you inhaled for the first time, He already wanted to spend forever with you. I know, I know. Eternity sounds like a long time, and there's a lot of living to do between now and then. However, He who knew the end before the beginning began has prepared the way for you. He lovingly walks with you. You are His, and He is yours, so be confident that the One who has begun such a marvelous work in your heart and life will see the work through until the end. Image is everything, and you were created to reflect His.

Chapter Fifteen
Solitary Sanctity

It's not popular, you know. Sanctification doesn't have widespread appeal. In a world where individuality looks less and less individual, who really wants to stand out? When you blend into the sea of identical uniqueness, pressure decreases. There is something alluring about mimicking reality TV personalities and music icons. Even when their lives are falling apart, they still look well put together. You can do the same by following the fad. Being different comes at a price; it draws attention that you would prefer not to receive.

If we live in the Spirit, let us also walk in the Spirit. Galatians 5:25

Imitation is the norm while stares, whispers, and often outright character bashing come to those who stand for a higher standard. Walking in the Spirit takes work. Obedience and diligence don't sound as appealing as favor and joy, but there *is* a connection. *And all these blessings shall come upon you and overtake you, because you have obeyed the voice of the Lord your God.* (Deuteronomy 28:2). Still, it seems easier to conform. Have you stopped to consider that you are destined to be different? Let's cut to the chase. How intimidating is it to be set apart for the sake of righteousness?

And do not be conformed to this world, but be transformed by the renewing of your mind, that you may prove what is that good and acceptable and perfect will of God. Romans 12:2

It is not by good intentions or willpower alone that you live this life, but by the Spirit of the Lord. Being different is a result of thinking differently, and that's highly doable because you have the mind of Christ. As the Holy Spirit ministers to your spirit, the seed of God's Word takes root in your heart and enables you to see the world through new lenses. Step by step, you're walking out the will of God. Day by day, you are being transformed into His image. Religion consumes you with lists of don't do's, but a continual pursuit of the presence of God causes those lists to fall away as you seek to know the depth, width, and height of His love. Holiness isn't about long skirts and hair buns. It's a heart matter.

13 Therefore gird up the loins of your mind, be sober, and rest your hope fully upon the grace that is to be brought to you at the revelation of Jesus Christ; 14 as obedient children, not conforming *yourselves to the former lusts, as in your ignorance; * [15] *but as He who called you is holy, you also be holy in all your conduct, * [16] *because it is written, "Be holy, for I am holy."* I Peter 1:13-16

This experience is relational. *If you love Me, you will keep My commandments.* (John 14:15). These aren't the words of a tyrant. Rest your hope on the grace that connected your heart to Christ. There is no whip cracking, but sin does lead to breaking. Disobedience breaks God's heart because it causes a disruption in fellowship. He only wants good for you, and it is promised that the fullness of all things good is found in His presence.

Understand this, "thus saith the Lord", is the same as, "so says the Father". The same God who requires obedience also says, *Enlarge the place of your tent, and let them stretch out the curtains of your dwellings; do not spare; lengthen your cords, and strengthen your stakes.* (Isaiah 54:2). Boundaries aren't bad. Wisdom leads to understanding and understanding produces growth. A renewed mind understands that the life with limits will experience limitless possibilities. Self-control is a fruit of the Spirit. It has been given for you to operate in the character of God while dodging the fiery darts of the one who comes to steal your joy, kill your dreams, and destroy your identity. Restrictions are for your preservation.

The life that is reined in is the life that reigns. You are called to be the head and not the tail, above and not beneath, the lender and not the borrower! We shout on that truth, but silence falls when it's mentioned that we are called to live sanctified lives. *Be holy for He is holy.* (1 Peter 1:16) Think on that with your renewed mind. Holiness is godliness, spiritual purity, and dedication to God. This is an intimidation-free zone so stop thinking in terms of mandated perfection. You aren't demanded to be this in your strength. The call to holiness is an opportunity to allow the Spirit of God to flow through you. See this concept through your new lenses:

I have been crucified with Christ; it is no longer I who live, but Christ lives in me; and the life which I now live in the flesh I live by faith in the Son of God, who loved me and gave Himself for me. Galatians 2:20

Sanctification isn't a scary summons; it is a promise of privileged positioning. You were created to be set apart. Don't dread being different. Embrace it. Truth be told, you will experience seasons of isolation. That's life. Consider it growing pains. Be that solitary star that shines in the midst of darkness. Soon enough the clouds will part and you will see you aren't shining alone. Stand out. Shine bright for the Son. Be sanctified.

Chapter Sixteen
Grand Finale

And if I go and prepare a place for you, I will come again and receive you to Myself; that where I am, there you may be also.
John 14:3

He promised to return. The trumpet will sound, the clouds will part, and you will *know* it was worth it. By faith, you have received salvation and surrendered your life. At the appearance of Christ, the reason for your hope will become reality. Then, you will be more certain than ever that this race has been worth it.

[51] Behold, I tell you a mystery: We shall not all sleep, but we shall all be changed—[52] in a moment, in the twinkling of an eye, at the last trumpet. For the trumpet will sound, and the dead will be raised incorruptible, and we shall be changed. [53] For this corruptible must put on incorruption, and this mortal must put on immortality.[54] So when this corruptible has put on incorruption, and this mortal has put on immortality, then shall

be brought to pass the saying that is written: "Death is swallowed up in victory." I Corinthians 15:51-54

Lord, thank You for Your faithfulness. You began a sanctifying work in Your daughter and will not remove Your hand until its complete. You are preparing her for joyfully ever after. At the coming of Christ, she shall be the glorified being that You imagined forever ago. She will be perfected in the presence of Perfection. This earthly experience exposes her to levels of glory, but eternity will introduce her to ultimate glorification as she worships at Your throne. She will join the angels in singing, *"Holy, holy, holy is the Lord God Almighty, Who was and is and is to come."* O, to worship at Your feet! There is no sweeter place than basking in the glow of Your glory. In love, You have offered her this everlasting sweetness. Thank You, Father. In love, she faithfully waits.

Princess, this world and all its imperfections shall pass away, but you shall remain. The corruptible will be exchanged for incorruptible, mortality for immortality. You have been promised unending goodness by the greatest Father there is. Keep hoping. Remain obedient. My sister, *let us not grow weary while doing good, for in due season we shall reap if we do not lose heart.* (Galatians 6:9). Every promise fulfilled today is a glimmer of hope for the ultimate promise that is to come. He promised to return.

Being confident of this very thing, that He who has begun a good work in you will complete it until the day of Jesus Christ. Philippians 1:6

[20] Now may the God of peace who brought up our Lord Jesus from the dead, that great Shepherd of the sheep, through the blood of the everlasting covenant, [21] make you complete in every good work to do His will, working in you what is well pleasing in His sight, through Jesus Christ, to whom be glory forever and ever. Amen. Hebrews 13:20-21

Christ will return. That's a Blood-bought, covenant promise. Until then, you are in the process of becoming complete in every good work to do His will. Sweetie, you aren't alone. The God of peace is with you. Do you understand the fullness of that statement? Peace is far more than tranquillity. Being derived from the Hebrew word *shalom*, it indicates wholeness. The God of wholeness is making you whole. He is completing you. The Father is mending every broken place and driving out every aspect of lack. God is not a God of voids. He is filling you to the point of overflow.

He is well able and willing to do *exceedingly abundantly above all that you can ask or think, according to the power that works in you.* (Ephesians 3:20). That power is the Holy Spirit. His flow of grace that affirms your position in the kingdom is continually transforming you into the likeness of Christ by way of sanctification and will seal the deal with glorification. God isn't just well intentioned; He is achieving His will both in and through you. Christ will return, but for now you are in process.

[56] The sting of death is sin, and the strength of sin is the law. [57] But thanks be to God, who gives us the victory through our Lord Jesus Christ. [58] Therefore, my beloved brethren, be steadfast, immovable, always abounding in the work of the Lord, knowing that your labor is not in vain in the Lord. I Corinthians 15:56-58

You are free from death, sin, and the law. *By grace you have been saved through faith.* (Ephesians 2:8). If the Lord tarries and you experience natural death, have no fear. It will merely be the catalyst that shifts you to the other side. You will pass from this life to everlasting life. A place has been prepared for you. He promised. For now, abound in the work of the Lord.

Dear Princess,

I urge you to live, *really* live while you're in process. You are rightly positioned, properly empowered, called for a purpose and fueled by faith in His promises. You are unstoppable, so step out of the way. Give God room to be God. Reflect the character of Christ as you walk in the Spirit. You are in Christ, and His Spirit is in you. Face each day thoroughly convinced of your divine lineage. Live like you know your Daddy. YOU ARE

ROYALTY. You were created to reign. Flow in your princess mentality daily.

Father,

Thank You for the opportunity to experience this journey with Your daughter. I pray that with the turning of each page, Your Word became more deeply rooted in her heart. May those roots spring up into trees of life as she bears much fruit for Your glory.

Lord, have Your way in the life of Your princess. I pray that her heart remains tender and her worship is always sincere. Renew her mind with the regenerating truth of Your Word. Fill her mouth with words of life. Steady her feet on the path of righteousness. When others see her, I pray they see You. And Lord, when she sees herself, I pray she sees herself through Your eyes.

Finally, Father, I pray that You bless and keep her. Smile upon her with gladness and continue to draw near to her and she draws near to You. In Jesus' name I pray. Amen.

Be blessed, boo!

Mentality Shift: Promise

Chapter Thirteen

What is currently the most pressing circumstance in your life? How can you choose to rest in Christ during this season?

Chapter Fourteen

Describe your "core" identity. What does this ordained version of you have to offer the world?

Chapter Fifteen

In what areas of your life has the Holy Spirit not been allowed
to reign?

Chapter Sixteen

What does living while in process look like for you?

Commitment to Reign

I, _____, believe that God the Son gave His life to bring me into right fellowship with God the Father and position me to be comforted, counseled, and led by God the Spirit. (Romans 8:12-17). I vow to live in a manner worthy of my calling (Ephesians 4:1), trusting Christ Jesus as the author and finisher of my faith (Hebrews 12:2). As a daughter of the King, I have a hope and a future. (Jeremiah 29:11). I confidently profess that I am His workmanship, created for good works. (Ephesians 2:10). Today, by the divine authority endowed to me, I declare that I am the head and not the tail, above and not beneath. (Deuteronomy 28:13). I am a daughter of the Most High, and I am ready to reign.

_____   _____
Signature   Date

About the Author

LaToya NaShae's passion and purpose are equipping others to live like they know WHOSE they are. This is accomplished through the avenues of writing, speaking, and coaching. She readily comes along beside others on their journey to discovering who they are in Christ and becoming empowered to walk in purpose. Whether publicly declaring the Good News of Christ or engaged in one-on-one coaching, LaToya walks with others along their journey of faith and freedom. Her aim is to encourage people to become unstuck in their minds, unbound in their lives, and unbreakable in their Christ-identity.

LaToya NaShae is a graduate of Murray State University and the Christian Coach Institute. She is the founder of BREAKOUT Coaching, where she walks with women on the journey to living unstuck, unbound, unbreakable lives in Christ!

Connect with LaToya NaShae

Facebook: Breakout-Coaching
Instagram: @coach_latoyanashae
YouTube: LaToya NaShae

www.ingramcontent.com/pod-product-compliance
Lightning Source LLC
Chambersburg PA
CBHW060301050426
42448CB00009B/1712